I'm More
than the Pastor's Wife

Lorna Dobson

I'm More
than the Pastor's Wife

*Authentic Living
in a Fishbowl World*

~ Revised Edition ~

ZONDERVAN™

GRAND RAPIDS, MICHIGAN 49530 USA

ZONDERVAN™

I'm More Than the Pastor's Wife
Copyright © 1995, 2003 by Lorna Dobson

Requests for information should be addressed to:

Zondervan, *Grand Rapids, Michigan 49530*

Library of Congress Cataloging-in-Publication Data

Dobson, Lorna, 1949–
    I'm more than the pastor's wife : authentic living in a fishbowl world / Lorna
Dobson.
      p.   cm.
    Includes bibliographical references.
    ISBN 0-310-24728-4
    1. Spouses of clergy.   I. Title.
    BV4395.D57   1995   94-45168

Interior design by Beth Shagene

Printed in the United States of America

---

06 07 08 09 /❖ DC/ 10 9 8 7 6 5

With gratitude to my husband,
Ed, who has always encouraged me to write.

Contents

Preface / 11

Chapter 1
The Bible: Your Only Blueprint / 19

Chapter 2
The Struggle for Balance: Keeping the Beam Low / 33

Chapter 3
Excess Baggage: Calculating the Cost / 49

Chapter 4
First Things First: Sorting the Laundry / 61

Chapter 5
Feeling Alone: Sharing in Christ's Suffering / 75

Chapter 6
Personal Stuff: Taking Care of Me / 93

Chapter 7
Mutual Submission: Partnering in Godliness / 115

Chapter 8
Enough Is Enough: Setting Boundaries / 133

Chapter 9
Husband Support: Being in His Corner / 145

Chapter 10
Support Group: Custom Designing Your Own / 161

Chapter 11
God's Glory: A Sure Calling / 169

Appendix: Resources / 179

Notes / 185

Preface

WHEN I BEGAN WRITING THE FIRST EDITION OF THIS BOOK ABOUT ten years ago, my children were still living at home. I had a strong desire to address everyday issues pastors' wives face. I couldn't state dogmatically just how parenting pastors' children should be done, only that sorting through the issues of living in a "fishbowl" was a continual challenge presenting a need for godly wisdom. I was young enough not to have faced every ministry crisis in our first twenty years that Ed and I might experience. I knew, however, that the journey of growing spiritually, of knowing God, was the most essential part of this life; and I wanted to impart my passion for that discipline to other ministers' wives. I'm still growing, both spiritually and emotionally, and learning more about ministering to people in the church as well as outside the family of God, serving with my husband and supporting him as a pastor. We are almost empty nesters now but with a larger family, having gained a daughter-in-law over four years ago and having been blessed with a granddaughter.

Because my own roles in the home have changed in relation to my children, I wanted to expand what I had written about making marriage a priority; none of us wants to be blindsided by a new season of life. Chapter 4 deals with some questions that have been raised as my husband, Ed, and I have worked on this issue.

Some of our answers have been found in discovering the beauty and challenges of being outdoors. As a couple and with our family, Ed and I have done more hiking, backpacking, canoeing, and camping in the last few years than in all the other years together. Getting unplugged refreshes us unlike anything else we've ever done. We appreciate each other's company more than ever, especially since the uncertainties of life became the focus when Ed was diagnosed in late 2001 with a motor-neuron disease medically called "probable ALS" (Lou Gehrig's disease). Ed's checkup in the fall of 2002 showed only slightly detectable signs of progression of the disease, for which we are thankful to the Lord. As this book goes to press, his neurologist is convinced Ed does not have the classic form of ALS, a degenerative, fatal disease for which there is no known cause or cure. The prayers of many people have uplifted us more than we can express. Our dependence on God for daily strength and wisdom is much more than a belief; it's a working reality. The joy of becoming grandparents during the months of strain and adjustment in many areas of our lives was a blessing as big and wonderful as every grandparent had ever told us it would be!

My heart was touched by the feedback from many who read the first edition. They indicated that the Lord used my addressing of common challenges to help ministry wives, as well as women not in full-time ministry, in specific ways. Some found strength to face their own identity crises, to address and change expectations they have had on themselves, or to deal with expectations others have put on them. With the passage of time, however, I sensed that I had more words of encouragement for pastors' wives. This became clearer to me when members of ministry wives' support groups and teachers of seminary students' wives told me the wives want to learn specific ways to support their husbands as spouses and as ministers. Therefore, in this updated edition, I have added a chapter addressing some ways ministers' wives can support their husbands (chapter 9) and a chapter on starting support groups for pastors' wives (chapter 10).

The issues pastors' wives and their families face are often the same as people in the congregation face, with some added pressures. Many people in our congregations live more difficult lives than we do; however, our commonalities related to our husbands' calling and occupation give us reasons to address issues unique to our lives. If there is abuse or immorality in the parsonage, not only is the clergy family in jeopardy, but their ministry, their calling, and the hearts and lives of their congregation hang in the balance. If their children rebel, ministry parents sometimes face the possibility of leaving the pastorate. And the growing number of couples entering ministry after years of marriage and professional work outside ministry face unique challenges that need specialized encouragement to fulfill their calling.

Because women whose husbands are in ministry often experience loneliness, particularly during personal or church crises, I offer resources for readers who need a place to turn for help. Updated information, resources, and books for further reading can be found in the appendix. Many more caregiving ministries are in existence now than ten years ago. The younger generation of pastors' wives will find many older ones who are willing to listen, support, and sometimes advise; this was not always so when I was young. Verbalizing issues and hearing from other ministers' wives the comforting words, "This, too, shall pass," has great value.

Times have become increasingly tougher in the thirty years since Ed and I entered ministry. Multiple career families, single- and divorced-parent issues, and blended families have increased, even among clergy. When I surveyed pastors' wives ten years ago, about 42 percent worked outside the home; I do not have current statistics, but I know that now, because of work factors, it is almost impossible to schedule meetings and support groups when everyone can attend. Ministry to burned-out and defaulted ministers and their families has escalated, while consumer-oriented and lawsuit-driven church-hoppers complicate ministry. People with HIV/AIDS in need of pastoral care and those who have experienced physical, emotional, or spiritual abuse add further to ministry responsibilities. Since September 11, 2001, people are exhibiting new fears. Many have lost jobs, and some are simply searching for spiritual answers to questions they had not previously asked. And although many of us go about our daily lives as if nothing has changed, our country is at war.

Part of my research for the first edition of this book involved sending out surveys to more than 230 women representing every state and four foreign countries. I received responses from women in twenty-nine states and all four countries. The 59 percent response indicated that there was, and I believe still is, a high level of interest in dealing with the issues ministers' wives face. Survey questions were derived from women I met in small groups, particularly at Leadership Network retreats and a renewal retreat ministry called Paraklesis, which Ed helped to begin. While some of the statistics might differ if the survey were taken today, the sampling of thoughts from pastors' wives helps us hear differing views as well as my own.

I cannot fully identify with every type of ministry situation, such as the dynamics of marriage in which both husband and wife are ordained and pastor separate churches or pastor the same church together, or in which the husband is a layperson and the wife is the minister. But for more than thirty years, I have been the wife of a man called to preach the gospel and teach the Word in many different ministry settings. Ed preached his first sermon in a jail and spent many hours street preaching in New York City. As newlyweds, we traveled as an evangelistic team. Ed interim-pastored several churches in metropolitan and medium-sized cities. We started a church in a small mountain town. Later Ed worked as an associate pastor, a Christian college administrator-teacher-coach, a Christian school board member, a writer, and an editor. And for more than fifteen years he has served as senior pastor at Calvary Church in Grand Rapids, Michigan. Through all these years, I have met many ministry wives who are looking for another's challenge to keep walking when the way seems rocky or slippery. They long to be encouraged to seek or to offer help when it is needed and to be given hope that they can find contentment, peace, and joy "whatever the circumstances" (Phil. 4:11).

I have read nearly every possible word combination for identifying ministry people. It is difficult to address issues related to "us" without using terms that are sometimes offensive to women who desire a separate identity. But since using a term such as *pastor's wife* is the only way to identify the subject of this book, I acknowledge that it is a "title" for a part of one's life that is not a career, a position, and for some, not even a calling or perceived role. Being the wife of a pastor is not a job.

Before you read further, please put aside all thoughts of your spouse for a few moments. Forget your hopes, dreams, and expectations. Forget your social status. Forget the impact on your life by your family of origin. Think only of your relationship to God, to his Son Jesus Christ, and to the indwelling Holy Spirit. If your sins have been forgiven through your faith in Christ's death on the cross on your behalf, extended by grace as the only way of salvation from an eternity of separation from God, giving you hope of eternal life because of his resurrection, then think of your place in his family and all that is yours for the asking—actually, for the taking of what is already offered to you. Now ponder only God himself—holy, gracious, compassionate, understanding, unchanging, good, slow to anger, rich in love, patient, merciful, righteous. He is your Comforter, Strength, Song, Deliverer, Rock, Shield, Creator, King, Father, Peace, Judge.

With that perspective you are ready to deal with the issues of life—your responsibilities to fellow believers as well as to those outside of God's family. Being a pastor's wife is not the biggest issue of life; living as God's child and handling circumstances in a manner pleasing to him is what matters. My hope is that you will be encouraged by reading this book.

Many thanks are due to the hundreds of ministry wives I have talked to through my first thirty years of ministry, whose stories may only be seen in this book as a statistic or an example. I am especially grateful to my friends, especially Judy DeVries and Linda Riley, who have accepted the call to minister to pastors' wives, because their help and support has enhanced my own spiritual health. Of course, it is only with the blessing of my husband, Ed, that I am free to expose some parts of our lives that might otherwise be kept private. Vulnerability, we have learned, opens doors to ministry. Therefore, we do not want to shrink from opportunities to help one another on this journey.

Chapter 1

The Bible

Your Only Blueprint

BRINGING UP THE ISSUE OF THE "ROLE" OF PASTOR'S
wife to some pastors' wives is like hitting a
land mine. Several women who responded to
my survey objected to my use of the word *role*
or felt that it is erroneous to assume that there is
such a thing as a role. Two wrote that they are "trying to be free from that," and more said that they
already felt free from "it." Many object to the term *min-*
isters' wives and feel that "'wives or spouses of ministers,'
or 'those married to pastors' seems more palatable since
each implies a certain distinctiveness of persons." A far
greater portion of the respondents are not bothered by
terms and have accepted them as the means of verbalizing the way life is or is not perceived. One of our
church staff wives says, "Anyone who is married
to someone in ministry should know and
accept the fact that there is 'stuff' that
goes with it!" Not everyone can
easily accept the "stuff."

Let Me Be a Lawyer's Wife

"The minister's spouse cannot be just another member of the parish. Everyone has some idea (usually a different one) of how the minister's spouse ought to behave and be involved in the parish. Clergy spouses face these projections all the time."[1] Imagine marriages with the husbands in a variety of professions: Would a client expect the attorney's wife to be in the courtroom, thereby eliminating doubt that the lawyer could be trusted to defend him/her satisfactorily because he is trusted by his spouse? Would the obstetrician's wife be expected to attend every delivery, or the surgeon's wife scrub so that she could be near her husband while he was under the pressure of performing surgery? Would the plumber's wife attend every pipe fitting? Would the pastor's wife be expected to go calling at all times with her husband even when they had three small children? Would she be expected to do office work, type the bulletin, direct the choir, and be an officer in the ladies' missionary society for no pay? Would she be expected to go out to Sunday dinner at the invitation of church members while leaving their children, ages six, nine, and eleven, at home?

Couldn't happen, you say? I doubt that it would for an attorney, doctor, or plumber, but the pastor and his wife alluded to above are real, faithful members of our present church, and the expectations listed touch only a tip of the iceberg. When they lived in one parsonage, they had to ask for permission to paint a room or to hang something on the wall. They were expected to entertain church members in their small home with no dining room and with very limited finances. Certain members complained because a porch light was left on during the evening service—the "Lord's money" was being wasted! A member walked into the parsonage one evening and informed the daughter that she should turn off the kitchen light—she was wasting electricity! That's enough cause for a normal person to want to be the spouse of anybody *but* a pastor!

This couple wrote on their survey questionnaire that "traditional, midsized, and small churches have unrealistic expectations of the pastor's wife and family. The board or members take it upon themselves to dictate their private lives. Small churches in particular have strong church traditions and preferences without biblical support when it comes to pastors' wives and families. She is often not allowed to be her own person."

The Struggle Is Not New

"A minister's wife has no more call to public duty than any Christian woman in the congregation." Sound like the twenty-first century? It was written in *The Diary of a Minister's Wife* over one hundred years ago. In the 1880s Lucy, the young wife of a minister, was told by her visiting cousin that she should take piano lessons so that she could play for church services; that way, if choir members quarreled, Lucy and her husband could sing and play and be "it," independent of such problems. Further, she insisted that the pastor's wife should be the president of the ladies' aid and missionary societies. But Lucy's husband replied:

> A minister's wife has no more call to public duty than any Christian woman in the congregation. In fact, he thinks she [the pastor's wife] ought never to hold such offices, because she is not a fixture and may leave the work just at a time when experience is a necessary factor to cope with circumstances, and the new officer might thus be put to disadvantage and the society suffer. Then, too, if she be capable and aggressive, some would say she wants to run everything, while if she is modest and self-deprecating and waits for others to suggest, these same fault-finders will say they hope the next minister's wife will be of some help to them.[2]

Some things never change. I have been told that I should teach or lead "people-oriented groups" and should not perform in choir or on keyboards. And I have also been told that I should give up my duties as choir pianist for a month to work in the nursery. In a church that we started after nine months of marriage, I was told that I should have a baby and settle down so the church would know we meant to stay. Others told me that

I should teach Sunday school. Thankfully, when I have turned to my husband for advice in these matters, he has said, "Do what you want to do." Since I was trained to play the piano, it was natural for me to do that for many years. Later in the book I will explain the process of breaking away from that to develop teaching and leading gifts.

Give Me a Break

Frances Nordland provides a "blueprint for the ideal preacher's wife" by way of a ludicrous "drawing of [a] composite creature" including every skewed idea one may have heard. The wording with the blueprint reads, "Available only with ideal preacher. We do not break a set!"[3] Further, she quotes a layman who has written one of the most stereotypical, old-fashioned, tongue-in-cheek bits I have read about the requirements for pastors' wives:

> Applicant's wife must be both stunning and plain, smartly attired, but conservative in appearance, gracious and able to get along with everyone, even women. Must be willing to work in the church kitchen, teach Sunday school, babysit, run multilith machine, wait table, never listen to gossip, never become discouraged.[4]

A counselor friend adds, ". . . yet be fully aware of all church problems so she might 'pray more intelligently.'"

As ridiculous as the above paragraph seems, many pastors' wives sometimes feel that everyone wants a piece of them or expects them to do more than they can handle. Since survey respondents gave so much advice about the worthlessness of trying to please everyone, about learning to say no, and about being all you need or want to be, we will look more closely at this advice later in the book. First, let us focus on who Christ wants us to be.

Have We Really Followed Biblical Teaching?

Only a few Scripture passages address the role of the wife of overseers (pastors/leaders) and deacons, but the few are powerful. First Timothy 3:11 says, "Wives are to be women worthy of respect, not malicious talkers but temperate and trustworthy in everything." While there is some controversy over interpretation of the original language regarding whether this passage is referring to deaconesses as officers in the church or to the wives of deacons, it appears to be applicable to women who have high visibility and influence in the church because of their "acts of kindness and of help and of charity which only a woman could properly do for another woman."[5] Wives of any kind of ministers are observed and therefore are role models for others.

Frances Nordland gives a practical solution for what ministers' wives should be like:

> We need to recognize that in the early church period the leaders of the church were men whom we would now designate as laymen. There was no separation, as now, between clergy and laymen, making a separate class of people in the church known professionally as "ministers." So, if you want to learn from the Bible what a minister's wife should be like, you must look for references to wives. You will find no double standard—one for the pastor's wife and one for the layman's wife.[6]

Paul's message to Timothy provides a godly basis for a weighty responsibility carried by the wife because of her husband's position and responsibility. Some women married to ministers balk at this connection. But what the Bible actually addresses here is the area of discretion and personal maturity, and not any specific duties she performs in the church. It is my observation that some of the balking may be due to a lack of biblical foundation regarding God's intended role, not as pastors' wives, but as women created to be "a helper suitable for him" (Gen. 2:18).

Not every wife of a minister feels pressure to be someone she isn't. Pastors' wives in nontraditional churches that target the unchurched say that traditional expectations generally are not an issue with them. They feel free to serve with their gifts as they are led by the Lord, because new Christians usually do not come into the church with a set of expectations for the staff and their spouses. Conversely, couples who serve small congregations steeped in tradition often find a binding code of spoken and unspoken expectations that will not be swayed by new vision.

A pastor's wife must give serious consideration to the "position" she is in—namely, as the "wife of" a man who has set his desires on a "noble task" (1 Tim. 3:1). The position carries with it the responsibility to manage his family in a way that will cause him to be worthy of respect. So whether we feel that we have chosen our lot in life or not, whether we want to call it a "role," or whether we will forever be frustrated by not being able to change the stereotypes people have held about us, our love for our husband and commitment to help him fulfill his own dreams is cause enough to spur us to seek a heart of contentment and peace within our circumstances.

Note that Paul admonishes both overseers and their wives to be "worthy of respect" (1 Tim. 3:2, 8, 11). Commentaries translate and rephrase the words "worthy of respect" (v. 11) as dignified, honorable, holy, or stately. "It is a positive term ... [that] denotes a seriousness of mind and character. [It] does not mean austere or unbending, however."[7] (See also Phil. 4:8; Titus 2:2, 7.)

Further, Paul warns against talking maliciously. If hurtful, loose talk is an area of weakness in your life, you will suffer from a reputation that will shadow you everywhere you go, and you likely will be a detriment or contribute to the ruin of your husband's public ministry. To remove yourself from this rut you can do what the psalmist did. He placed his sinful problems under God's control and prayed, "Keep your servant ... from willful sins; may they not rule over me. Then will I be blameless, innocent of great transgression" (Ps. 19:13). We can guard against loose talking by adopting a concentrated, disciplined lifestyle of Scripture memory. While God can and will forgive us of our sins of the tongue when we repent, we need to fill our minds and hearts with his Word, for it is "out of the overflow of the heart" that the mouth speaks (Matt. 12:34).

Paul's admonition for pastors' wives to be temperate has been interpreted different ways by congregational members. To be temperate means to be marked by moderation, not extreme or excessive. The problem lies in the varieties of ideas congregations have regarding the areas in which a pastor's wife should be temperate. Thus, we have the basis for the impossible blueprint. For example, in the area of clothing, some may say her style of dress is too showy while others say it is outdated. Extreme hairdos and clothing styles are to some "flashy" yet to others "classy." Excessive makeup may be defined as "ready for TV" by some but as lip gloss and clear nail polish by others. Paul, however, was using the word *temperate* to refer to more than outward appearance; he was alluding to a gracious spirit not given to extremes or overreaction.

Finally, Paul calls wives of overseers to be trustworthy in everything. A trustworthy wife may not be able to do everything, but she is dependable for whatever she pledges her word. The requirement is for "thorough-going 'reliability' . . . [and] holds for women as well as elders and deacons."[8] The virtuous woman of Proverbs 31 is a good example of trustworthiness. We read that she never gives her husband cause to doubt the strength of her character or her commitment to him.

Peer Pressure in Ministry?

Another avenue of life that complicates the identification of the role is an unwritten code of ethics in the ministry by which peers are judged and assumptions are made. This code involves such issues as what to wear and who to associate with. Ruthe White states a general biblical principle to be used as a guide:

> While it may be true that our roles have never been clearly defined, and no church denomination (at least to my knowledge) has set down any clear-cut do's and don'ts for the clergy, we are not exempt from the Golden Rule, "Do unto others as we would have others do unto us." Living by this principle is not always easy, not even in the parsonage. Matthew, Mark, and Luke recorded these words of Jesus:

'If anyone wants to be a follower of mine, let him deny him- and take up his cross and follow me. For anyone who keeps his life for himself shall lose it; and anyone who loses his life for me shall find it again" (Matt. 16:24, 25; see Mark 8:34; Luke 9:23, TLB).[9]

Gulp. Deny myself? The point the author is making is that ministry couples who obey this principle "have to risk being misunderstood ... [and] will be called upon ... to bring about a breach in ministerial relationships. We are often 'pitted' one against the other."[10] These breaches alone expend years of many ministry lives and detour the followers whose mission is to tell others how to be followers. Although some ministry people feel called to crucify their peers by broadcasting judgment labels, that kind of name-calling should play no part in our supportive ministry.

Who Trains the Pastor's Wife?

We have our own set of expectations about our role as wives of ministers. We have another set of what we think the congregation expects of us, a set from our husband, and another from the church board. Fortunately, we can discuss these issues with our husband, and he should discuss expectations with the church board. Then we can try to balance perceptions with reality.

Another factor that plays heavily on us is what our mentors said—or did not say—to us in preparation for life in the ministry. About 18 percent of survey respondents said that they had no preparation for becoming a minister's wife (that is, no mentors). One wrote, "There is a lack of training for pastors' wives; it is on-the-job training with training being expectations of people." Many others commented that although they received no formal education for life in ministry, other factors did help to prepare them. These included the positive impact of parents or future in-laws already in ministry, the role modeling of their own pastors' wives, solid Bible teaching, their own spiritual development and involvement in church during their youth, their commitment to their husband's being in ministry, the support of close

friends who were pastors' wives, and the support and p
relatives.

Along with 55 percent of the women surveyed, I felt a specific "call" to enter full-time ministry before I was married. I was
eager to follow any leading of the Lord, married or not.
However, at Bob Jones University, where I was attending, there
was no formal opportunity for preparation to be the wife of a
minister unless one was already married or officially engaged (I
missed that by a few months).

Instead, shortly after our marriage God allowed us to stay in
a home that gave us practical experience, although we did not
realize the full value of it for years. We house-sat a boxer for
three months while her owners went to Europe. Living in the
oldest, wealthiest section of town, we were given full privileges
and use of everything in the home with two servants, who did
anything for us we wished, just as if we were the owners of the
house. We were exposed to the richest and the poorest of the
community and learned that there is no difference in human
beings: they all have the same needs. We were not intimidated
by the wealthy (although we were somewhat in awe of their pos-
sessions!), nor did we feel that we were better than the poor ones
who waited on us.

I wish I could have had in hand at that time the kind of information I later received from Linda Riley, a pastor's wife and
writer. No matter what your preparation or lack of it, she has
provided a few practical thoughts to help you make choices for
involvement in ministry as you settle into your place in the parsonage and church life. Linda urges pastors' wives to "know how
you work in general." (If you are too young to be sure of that,
some trial and error will teach you, as it has us older women!)
Know your talents, interests not yet developed, whether you
enjoy following or leading, whether you do better one-on-one or
with a crowd. Know your capabilities and limits; if you are rais-
ing toddlers or battling disease, public ministry is limited.[11] And
if you are totally consumed with the lives of teenagers in your
home, remember what Patty McGinnis, our director of Women's

Ministry at Calvary, told me many years ago: "There will always be conferences and retreats and events for you to attend, but you only get one chance to be involved in your children's lives, and you'd better not miss that opportunity."

The only evidence of concrete ministerial preparation I can find from my own past is a list I had written on notebook paper. The source is unknown; I cannot remember where or when I wrote it. I agree with some of the points and have placed some candid comments after most of them. Some of them begin with "Don't," which I think is a poor way to train anyone for ministry!

1. Don't neglect personal devotions.
2. Don't forget your high calling and responsibility as first lady of the church. (I cringe when I hear the term "first lady," because I do not deserve more respect than other godly women. Nevertheless, this term is widely used in some ministerial circles.)
3. Back your husband completely in his work. Be a team. (Not every church wants two for the price of one; backing your husband does not mean that you have to appear at every church function; more on that in other chapters.)
4. Don't be a cold and unresponsive wife to your husband. (I wouldn't think of it!)
5. Don't be dictatorial. (Good thought for any leader!)
6. Show an obvious affection and interest in all members. (*Obvious* is a strong word and is easier to write than to live.)
7. Live peacefully with all kinds of people. (This is biblical but is hard to live out among whiners and constant callers.)
8. Cheerfully live within the family income. (About 10 percent of the women surveyed found this to be a difficulty and would like to see changes made in their finances.)
9. Keep strict confidences. Don't betray them.
10. Always use good common sense. (Mine is not always available!)

11. Have a sense of humor. (But you don't have to be the church clown.)
12. Let your husband give time to the Lord's work without resentment or complaint. (More on that in the following chapters.)
13. Have a pleasing personality.[12]
14. Be properly groomed at all times. An expensive wardrobe is not necessary. ("Properly" is where many differ.)
15. Keep a neat home, but don't be a slave to it. (This, too, is relative.)
16. Don't cause strife among church people by talking about some to others.
17. Don't argue or talk back to people. (That, too, will cause strife; however, every church would benefit from every member practicing numbers 1, 6, 7, 9, 16, and 17.)
18. Don't be too involved with people—that is, avoid having "special friends." (See chapter 6.)
19. Know your Bible. (I have been working on this my whole life, but I am still learning. Since I have not attended seminary, I sometimes feel intimidated by women who have.)
20. Don't get depressed. Display joy. (Does this mean "don't be real"?)
21. Keep your mind alert. Be up-to-date on current events. (I see value in this, but there are days when I can barely get through the mail and information sent home from three schools, church activities, and extracurricular activities. Number 1 is more important.)

Not All Advice Is Taken as Intended

A young mother once approached me almost in tears. She was attractive, and she and her children were well dressed; she and her husband made a handsome couple. He was studying for the ministry after having spent some years in business. She was eager to be part of that and did not object to the change, but she had just heard in a wives' support group emceed by the wife of one of his teachers that she had to keep a perfect-looking home. "I try to keep my home neat, but if it has to be perfect, I'll never make it as a pastor's wife!" I encouraged her to live in her home and lighten up about her own and others' expectations.

A few weeks later the teacher's wife who had emceed the group stopped by my house unannounced just after my toddler had emptied the cupboards and was sitting in the Dutch oven in the middle of the kitchen floor! There was no way to hide it all since the front door of our log cabin was next to a seven-foot window; there was no entryway to meet her away from the mess. I laughed inside, tried hard not to make excuses, but told her on the phone several weeks later that it was too bad she couldn't have stopped by at 10:30 P.M. on the same day she visited. By then everyone was in bed and I had picked up the day's leftovers in the great room and kitchen.

Now that I am older and a bit wiser, I realize that I should have sent the future ministry wife back to her mentor for a private conversation, where she would learn that she had misinterpreted what was said. I took her interpretation at face value instead of clarifying the issue myself, but I felt that because of my youth I would be perceived by the teacher as impertinent or just the type who needed that kind of teaching. The truth is, only recently have I cleared up the matter and learned what was intended to be conveyed: Our homes are a testimony, which should at least show that we care enough to be good stewards of the material things we have. Sometimes we are visited by people who just want to see how we live. If at all possible, we should try to keep the entryway or most-likely-to-be-seen room clean and neat.

We would all have been in agreement if we had taken the time to discuss the issue.

The Only Valid Blueprint

More important than the lists of expectations, which are easily misunderstood, is that we live according to God's blueprint, the Bible, which is our guide for living, just as it is for every

Christian. What people should see in our lives is that we are striving honestly to live out our faith.

Erin, a high school student, was giving a report to our church on her part in a summer ministry team to Kenya. She had been shocked at the intense interest the Kenyans had in her skin color; when white Americans appeared in a group, the black Kenyans stopped everything to look at the visitors. Erin tried to get used to it but was unable to do so. Then she began thinking about how things were at home in Michigan. People watched her at work, at home, at school, and even when she was driving her car—not because her skin color may have been different from their own, but because everyone watches other people's lives. How she acted at any time reflected her testimony as a Christian. She came home with a renewed sense of her desire to have a good testimony for the Lord, knowing that people were watching her life.

When I heard Erin speaking, I couldn't help but think that my life should be the same. How I live has little to do with whether my husband is a pastor; rather, my life reflects my growth, or lack of it, as a Christian. It speaks through the actions of love and compassion, or of bitterness and anger, I have toward God and people. If my desire is to know, love, and please the Lord, and my security is in him as his child, I will concentrate more on conforming my behavior to his standards so that others will want to know him. This will lead to a more peaceful life than if I am trying to do a list of things I think others expect of me.

With all that contemplated, I know that many people will still see me as and refer to me as "the pastor's wife." Whether my actions reflect God's character, a sinful one, or a confused mixture of the two, people will take note of "the pastor's wife" and judge me. Whether they are right or wrong, I will be held accountable to God for my actions and they for their judgments. If my actions cause them to stumble spiritually, that is a more serious matter to me, and I will be judged accordingly. My desire is for my character to be conformed to glorify God so that others will not stumble because of my actions or attitudes.

Action Points

- When making decisions, do you generally wonder first, "What will people in the church think?" If so, begin a new practice this week.
  1. Keep a journal of such thoughts, asking God to help you gain balanced perspective.
  2. Search the Scriptures for any clear teaching regarding the matter you must decide.
  3. Work in unity with your husband, especially if the matter will affect him or the family.

- If you feel that you lack training for your role as a minister's wife, set a realistic goal for the next year.
  1. Read available resources for pastors' wives.
  2. Attend one conference or retreat for pastors' wives.

Chapter 2

The Struggle
for Balance
Keeping the Beam Low

SOON AFTER OUR DAUGHTER BEGAN LEARNING
gymnastics, she was taught to walk the balance beam. A beginner's balance beam is
only six inches above the floor. The children
walk forward, then backward, later turn on it, roll,
and do a landing off it. A friend pointed out to me
that some of the children were forced to begin work on
a forty-eight-inch-high balance beam before they were
ready. When we saw fear registering on their faces and
learned that the teachers didn't care, my friend and I
decided to take our girls to a place that didn't force the
next step. Fear of the height itself or of the consequences
of falling sometimes causes a child to want to quit. A
coach sensitive to those fears would direct the child to
another type of routine or piece of equipment until
the child gained confidence.

Life has been like that for me at times.
My husband and I were both twenty-
three when we started a

church; the anticipation and excitement of the core group gave room to us novices for slips on the beam. After the church had become established and we bought our first home nearby, I felt closed in, as if I were teetering on the high beam with no coach or spotters. I was afraid of not being the right kind of person, not doing the right things; and I wanted to quit even though I knew I would not. Now, at more than twice that age, I know that others experience similar struggles.

"Most all of life is a struggle for balance. Contentment comes in knowing struggle is normal," one ministry wife wrote to me. More women identified this struggle as the most frustrating area of their role in ministry; closely tied to and identified with that struggle were the expectations of others and of themselves. About 54 percent of the women who completed a rating scale of contentment in their lives ranked quite content to very content in the area of their schedules; 46 percent were middle-of-the-road to less content, and one noted that "definite changes are being implemented due to some frustrations." Sometimes we just need a "spotter," a mature individual to encourage us to do something about those frustrations that give us the feeling that we're teetering off the beam with no pad on the floor below.

As I met with and surveyed ministers' wives, I heard struggles and challenges repeated: "Who am I?" (balancing their identity with and apart from their husband's occupation); "What can I do to balance schedules, expectations, criticism, and friendships?" With the common need for reassessing areas of our lives that require balance, let's look at these issues.

What's Your I.D.?

Many women who are married to pastors, evangelists, missionaries, or other Christian leaders feel that they are a part of a team, partners in ministry, thus relishing the identity that their husband's name connotes. Of the women I surveyed, 51 percent said they have "no problem" with being identified as "Pastor _____'s wife." They made such statements as, "I am secure in who I am," or "It was a problem when I was younger, but now that I'm more secure in who I am as a child of God, *role* doesn't matter." Furthermore, 22 percent of that number who are comfortable with such identification consider it an honor to be part of a team.

Recently I passed a church with a sign outside that stated the names of the pastors, a husband and wife. I have read about other ministry couples who are both pastors of their churches and liken themselves to Aquila and Priscilla in the Bible. Other couples who feel that marriage and ministry are a partnership, but don't necessarily use the title *pastor* for the wife, are indeed serving the Lord together. Even though I have always been active in the church, it has only been in recent years since I have not had constant care of children to occupy my time, that my husband and I have felt we could do more ministry together. I have maintained through the years that prayer is a great part of my ministry with and for Ed. I discuss this further in another chapter.

While about half the ministry women I surveyed are comfortable with their identity being tied to their husband's occupation, the other half struggle in varying stages and at different times with such a role identification. Jill Briscoe offers suggestions for women who are bothered by being called the "pastor's wife" or "missionary's wife." In the first place, she says, people who use this label for you usually mean no harm and are saying that you are somebody special; however, if you are offended by it, you may lovingly confront and let them know how you feel about the label.[1] One pastor's wife who completed my survey said that she had visited our church on vacation and overheard several women talking about me; they didn't use my name, but instead used the term "pastor's wife." The woman realized that they were expressing love for me, and this helped her sift through her own frustrations in identity.

Sometimes Even I'm Confused

Several women noted on the survey that the label may be a visitor's only way of connecting the man in the pulpit with a real family. Who can blame a person for wanting to know more about another individual? After all, we don't want to be ignored or forgotten (see chapter 5). As one woman wrote on her survey, pastors' wives do sometimes change their minds about whether they want to be identified alone or with their husband's occupation.

For example, while I love my husband, enjoy being with him more as time goes by, and feel at peace with our life-calling, there are times when I, as well as some women who completed the survey, cringe from being introduced as "Pastor Dobson's wife," because the ensuing conversation reveals that the person I meet thinks I'm strange, or doesn't care to know me as a person, or puts up a wall. About one-fourth of the respondents made statements to the effect that they would rather be introduced just by name, as a friend, and would rather be known as a "regular person." For those who work outside the home, having an identity in a workplace fulfills a need.

Although I had been content to be "the pastor's wife," I wondered if I had harbored a need for another identity. A few years ago I was able to "test the waters" to see if I really wanted to teach English to high school students, something I had registered in my mind as a nagging thought. I knew I did not want to return to teaching piano (I quit when my older children were three and seven), but I could not seem to shake this thought. My English teachers had a profound impact on my life, and something within me thought I either could or should do the same. I did some substitute teaching so that I could be with students, read the textbooks, and find out what was involved in teaching besides showing up with a lesson plan. It didn't take me long to realize that at fifty-plus I did not want to go back to school for two years to become certified, did not want to teach full time, and certainly did not want to grade papers every night! What I thought I wanted to do for many years wasn't reality.

Having a home-based business can be fulfilling as well. Frankly, when I wrote the first edition of this book, I failed to mention that I have worked several businesses throughout our marriage. The simplest reason for my failure to mention it is that

I did not really see it as a "job" to be written about, partly because I had kept it discreetly hidden from most people in our church so as not to appear to be a "salesperson." Now I have worked through those fears, realizing that I cannot help but share good information with people I care about. The story is told in another section of the book.

A Little Sensitivity Goes a Long Way

When I was new in the community in which I now live, my friend Gail told me that she would always introduce me by my name. If the person I met found out in conversation what my husband does for a living, that was our own business. I appreciated that as a gesture of sensitivity. She knew that some people who are introduced to the wife of a minister impulsively make statements like, "Oh, I'll have to be good now," or they give you the once-over to see if you are properly attired for the image. There is no easy way (or perhaps no way at all) to change the stereotypes of ministers' wives in people's minds; but these situations can offer us an opportunity to "show a gracious spirit."[2] I can keep that in perspective when I remember an anonymous quote I wrote in a prayer journal years ago: "When you consider how hard it is to change yourself and your own ways, think how nearly impossible it is to change others."

Struggling with Maintaining Identity in Widowhood

Looking further into the matter of our identification with our husband's occupation, we should consider those women who are left alone when their husband dies. A longtime friend of mine, Carol Gregory, a pastor's wife for many years, began a ministry to widows when her husband was executive director of the Independent Fundamental Churches of America. This ministry to widows of pastors was named Chera (Gk., "widow") Fellowship. Many of these women have no identity other than being ministers' wives. When their husbands die they are left virtually homeless and churchless and need to find their own identity and a place of ministry alone if they so choose. The ministry has grown to include widowers as well as widows whose husbands were not in ministry. Now in their "retirement," Carol has been able to take this ministry to Russia. She and her husband, Dick, are still very actively engaged in ministry.

I know one widow whose daughter says that her mother continues in her ministry as "pastor's wife" even though the mother lives in a new town and attends a church her husband never pastored; he passed away many years ago! This woman is an effective minister to many, but her family may fail to realize that she is not perceived as a "pastor's wife." In conversing with Carol about wives' and widows' struggles for identity, I gleaned this insight from her: If your heart attitude is right with God and you are willing to be used no matter what your circumstances are, he will open doors so that you can stand on your own. Isn't that true of any facet of our Christian walk?

The Meaning Behind the Label

While some ministry wives contend that others wouldn't introduce them as the "plumber's wife" if their husbands were plumbers, neither would those people have the same emotional and spiritual attachment to a plumber as to a pastor. When my husband stands with a family by the bedside of a loved one who has just died or by parents who hold a stillborn baby, when he performs a marriage ceremony, when he dedicates babies and their families to the Lord, he knows—even though he does not like to admit it—that people are touched by his presence and what he represents. He would prefer that people see him on the same level, at the foot of the cross, a sinner saved by grace. However, he realizes that the place of service he has accepted from God automatically puts him in a position often referred to in Christian circles as "undershepherd." Some denominations give pastors a label that elevates their position much higher.

Richard Neuhaus addresses this phenomenon in *Freedom for Ministry*. "There is an unspoken understanding that the minister does in a very powerful way represent and embody the community's ministry."[3] Albeit mystical or indescribable, people hold dear the words of comfort and challenge that their pastor offers during memorable times. Neuhaus continues, "One's being there is in a powerful sense the 'presence' of the Church, and of Christ. Why is it so urgently, so pathetically, important that the pastor be there? Because he is the palpable sign of the supportive community and the community's Lord."[4]

Because I am not with my husband all the time, I cannot enter emotionally into every situation he enters. Sometimes I choose not to bear the burdens of others with him because our children's activities seem so overwhelming that I cannot handle both. However, if I choose to detach myself totally from his ministry except in the cases of people I want to consider myself close to, or if I continually struggle for self-actualization and identity, I may do a disservice to his ministry and lose an opportunity for God to work in me as a developing Christian. I dare not chance the hindrance on the path toward Christlikeness. By detesting or shunning the connotation of the term *pastor's wife,* I may miss the chance for a more intimate marriage when my best friend is emotionally drained.

All people, including pastors' wives, want to be liked for who they are, not for a label, and not for their use in advancing another's cause. However, for a pastor's wife to deny that she is identified with her husband's work or to try to "fix" everyone's thinking to her liking is a waste of energy. We all would do well to take ourselves less seriously and to ease our demands for recognition. It is far better to look for the humorous side of people's reactions toward your identity and to realize that you may have the wrong perception of what others think you should be.

Balancing Schedules

Sometimes I feel pretty much in control of my routine, or at least that I don't have far to fall if I make a mistake. At other times I feel as if the beam has been jacked up to four feet without my realizing it. Since I am afraid of heights, I must keep demands at a controllable level; I want to be in command of how much I think I can handle so that I can factor in flexibility for that which enters my life unexpectedly. When my children were in three schools, I wanted to be involved in their lives and know the parents of their friends. Now as a mother, mother-in-law, grandmother, and pastor's wife, I still have to carefully sift with Ed the requests for our time related to church and parachurch activities (Ed's secretary and I work very closely on this).

As pastors' wives, what we need to realize is that our struggle for normalcy and balance is no more difficult than that of others. I spent a morning years ago working on a PTA project with three women: one ran a business, one took care of her own children as well as the troubled children of a relative, and another was active in community work and child care.

Our conversation drifted to the frustration of trying to make eating together as a family a priority, and I learned that their husbands' schedules were as difficult as that of my husband. A series of funerals seems to come in waves of inconvenient times, or my husband is called out to the hospital in the middle of the night, but the wife of a fireman deals with similar inconvenience. The fireman has to drop everything and move or a life may be lost. Since September 11, 2001, we have sadly realized more than ever before that the fireman's life may be lost as well. My husband also has to drop everything and meet the family in trauma; periodically our whole family is involved. Since such situations are beyond our control, the only way we can keep things in balance is to keep the beam low and try not to take on more daily activities than we can handle physically and emotionally, allowing for unexpected situations and making time for personal spiritual growth.

Make Use of Available Helps

While much of our lives is consumed with the urgent rather than the important, we can relieve the tension caused by looking down from the high beam by experimenting with creative ideas. This may mean dropping some of our own rigid expectations. I practiced this when I invited all of the visiting missionaries from an annual missions convention to come to our home for lunch. In past years I had cooked a wonderful meal, but this time life was piled too high. My husband's suggestion that we order pizza caught me before I fell off the beam. For dessert we cut up apples and dipped them in ready-made caramel dip. This was a turn-around on the beam for me, because I am one who thinks that only homemade food is worth serving. I had even swallowed my pride the day before and asked my neighbor to help me clean the main floor of the house because I couldn't handle it alone. I felt as if I floated through that landing off the high beam![5]

We Should Do This, We Should Do That

Closely related to schedule is what ministry women refer to as expectations—those of others, husband, and self. Expectations have much to do with how a ministry wife balances her time and uses her talents.

A pastor's wife whose spirit had been broken told me that before her husband accepted the call to a church, she had asked the board what was expected of her, but after the "honeymoon," those expectations were thrown out, and confusing messages began to blast at her from all sides. She sincerely desired to serve the Lord and to be a good mother, but people were viciously destroying her will to serve. During seven years of such strife, she learned that some church members had a history of running people off from their tightly woven group. She has spent years recovering from their abuse.

Before my husband took his present church, the chairman of the board asked him what my expectations would be upon arrival. Ed told him that I wanted to find my way around town and to figure out where the children belonged. Once we settled, I would find an area of service for which I was suited, probably in music. For the first six months I did nothing but attend until a minister of music was hired. He asked me to be the choir pianist based on my reputation as an accompanist for other choir direc-tors he knew. I began playing with the stipulation that I would stay committed to it only if it worked for the whole family. I did not play for every service or accompany every soloist or group. After twelve years, I resigned, believing it was time to be available for involvement in other forms of ministry, although I was not sure what that would mean. The process of accompanying, particularly playing the vocal parts in rehearsals, had become boring to me. I believe that when God is trying to get my attention to make a change, he uses the mundane things of life. I journaled about this process of prying my fingers off the keyboard for two years; when I finally said yes to God, I felt freedom unlike any I thought possible. I had relinquished the fear of losing my talent as well as giving up the identity I had in being a musician. My newly acquired freedom allowed me more time to minister with my husband, who had always supported me and my commitment to the music ministry. I had to base the decision on what I felt God wanted me to do, not on the expectations of humans.

After I was well into the initial process of writing this book, I risked my mental and emotional health by asking our church board what their expectations of the pastor's wife are, and whether over the years those expectations had changed. Having received two-thirds of the thirty elders' and deacons' responses, with only two unsigned (perhaps because they were critical of my participation in music ministry), I am pleased to say that the majority had biblically based priorities, as mentioned in chapter 1. Top priority is the relationship to God and responsibility to family, with great "latitude as to what she should *do*." None of them felt that the pastor's wife should attend every service, and one even stated, "Anyone who judges by those standards is thinking pretty shallow." She should not be "the church's bellhop, force her children to participate in every activity, perform as unpaid staff, be an 'enabler' for her spouse, be the bearer of the congregation's wishes, or limit her service only to the church if her gifts lie in other areas of service more appropriately met by parachurch or local service organizations," they said. Because the board is actively involved in how the pastor uses his time, both ministerially as well as for personal health and growth, they feel that his wife should have input into those discussions. For example, I periodically attend meetings with a small group of former board members who have become Ed's accountability group to discuss Ed's challenges and balance issues. They are godly men who love Ed and pray faithfully for him and for our family.

Another board member stressed the political considerations of the church as a community and the need for the couple to have a clear understanding with the board. He expressed a major concern by saying, "Unfortunately, if the level of involvement of the pastor's spouse falls below that of the committed church member of equivalent age and family situation, the congregation could view the spouse as being less than fully committed to the spouse's ministry." I knew he was just stating the principle, not speaking about my personal involvement.

Learning to handle expectations is a continuing process that requires communication with your spouse, the board, and sometimes with individuals who need to hear your heart for ministry as well as to hear you say no.

I Don't Mean to Be Critical, But . . .

Closely related to the need for balance is the influence of criticism in our lives. Honest criticism should be heard thoroughly, interpreted clearly, and taken seriously, especially when given in a kind spirit, because we may need to make changes. However, not all criticism is constructive. Critics who knowingly or ignorantly vocalize with a haughty spirit seldom get any point across except their attitude, and about all they accomplish is wearing down the spirit of the servants they are criticizing. They see only the part of the picture they want to see, and it is clouded by their own background.

Women who have been deeply hurt by cruel treatment and destructive criticism of parishioners develop a fear for service with their husbands and begin to shut down emotionally out of self-protection. Several wrote that their greatest frustration in ministry was that those for whom they expend the most effort seem to be the quickest to be disloyal, or worse, the least spiritually minded. I have wondered if this is one of the reasons why some older women in ministry are not available to younger women seeking their mentorship; they remember more bad times than good and will not bring them back into the open for inspection.

In any church there are usually a few negative people who feel called to vocalize their "concerns." In a large work, several may emerge vocally on more than one front, while others with expertise in certain fields offer helpful behind-the-scenes hints of dissatisfaction, developing pockets of support. The size of the church determines the proportionate number of complainers and underminers.

It is very difficult for the minister and his wife not to become cynical when he receives critical comments, especially if extended times of prayer and planning have preceded the object of criticism so as not to disobey any biblical directives. Even with realistic, healthy outlooks on life and ministry, we can easily become weary in well-doing when bombardments relentlessly strike from within the church family. Wives find it difficult to bolster their husbands when parishioners are on the offense. Criticism has shoved many ministers and their wives off the beam.

The Pastor's Dilemma

A problem many ministers face is this: How much criticism should I share with my wife in order to gain her support but not leave her with bad feelings about certain people? A minister may feel that he should be the all-American macho, handling stress alone, letting his wife think that everything at work is fine, or at least that he can handle it.[6] He may reason that if he shares with his wife some criticism he has received, she may dwell on that for months and detest the sight of the person who leveled the criticism at her husband. Danger lies in the husband sharing the criticism but then forgetting to tell the wife until weeks later that the issue has been resolved. He finally says, "Oh, honey, I forgot to tell you that Henry apologized for his negative attitude. We talked it all out, and he is really very supportive." Although the issue had been resolved for some time, the unknowing wife was still simmering. Even then it may be difficult for her to "let it go" since she played no part in the resolution. The balance that comes in open communication between husband and wife is very important. She does not want to be the last to know what is happening in her husband's life, and he needs to continually be learning about his wife's ways of dealing with criticism. (I address the matter of pastors' wives criticizing their husbands in another chapter.)

Let's Get Back to the Bible

If you are living with seemingly unresolvable problems created by the stress of criticism, do a check of these factors:

1. Inspect the situation to discern any disobedience to scriptural principles.
2. Determine your heart attitude toward the situation and persons involved.
3. Try to apply scriptural principles of resolution.
4. Maintain open communication with your spouse.
5. Come to terms with who you are and what you are gifted to do, as well as with your limitations.

If all of these are tried, tested, and still unresolved, study 1 Peter 3:13–18. Verse 17 says, "It is better, if it is God's will, to suffer for doing good than for doing evil." As servants of Christ, we continually learn that all in life is not what we consider to be fair (see chapter 5), but we place our hope in the knowledge that God sees, cares, and keeps accurate records of situations and will someday, as the righteous Judge, make things right. Whatever we endure can hardly be compared to what Christ endured for us.

Whom Do We Trust?

Balancing friendliness with friendships is an area with which wives of ministers must deal. Some are hurt or betrayed by

---

church members they thought to be friends. Nearly half of the women I surveyed say they feel a frustration in changing or developing friendships because of their husband's occupation.

The question of whether the pastor's wife should have close friends in the parish has been debated much to the dissatisfaction of many. Making decisions about friendships requires never-ending wisdom. One pastor's wife said she didn't see why it was such an issue, because she was too busy to develop new or keep up with old friendships. I come from the opposite viewpoint and fail to see how she could keep from working on at least some friendships, feeling that some day in the future she will wish she had some acquaintances who know her below the surface.

A good defense of friendships appears in *Renewal on the Run,* in which Jill Briscoe cites the circles of Jesus' friends: one special friend, three close friends, the chosen Twelve, and seventy close acquaintances. Briscoe says Jesus "never apologized for his friendships," and he "modeled friendship because he chose to need it and knew that we all needed it, too."[7]

Whenever I hear that couples preparing for ministry are taught not to be too involved with special friends, my gut feeling is that this is illogical. If the Bible says to "love one another deeply" (1 Peter 1:22), then one must acknowledge that surface relationships do not love deeply, nor do they hold the loved one accountable. It is not enough to tell churchgoers to practice this principle and not live it out in our own lives!

It is important, especially for those who realize that they need a few close friends, to use wisdom in choosing who their friends are and for what purpose. Some women confide in others things that should be kept confidential in the marriage; however, if the marriage communication is truthful and intimate, the practice of making and being friends is not so difficult.

I have always had some friends from my distant past who, until email became part of our lives, were not connected to what I do daily. They were very helpful in allowing me to escape for a laugh or just for a change. A few ministry friends live far from us, and they also provide a different level of understanding.

When you serve in a small community and church, it is important to have friends outside the church who have known you for a long time and to whom you can turn in times of need. A good time to establish lifelong friends is in seminary. Try to keep in contact with several couples once you launch out into ministry. If you are already established in ministry and did not make close friendships with other ministry couples earlier, begin a support group for local pastors' wives. I say more about this in another chapter.

I am not suggesting that you cannot befriend women in a small church, but there is potential for misunderstandings in a small setting when exclusivity of friendships is more visible than in a larger church community. Your dependence on friends within the church can be a source of hurt if it is your only source. That potential exists even in our church, because four generations of some families have married each other; after fifteen years I'm still learning of family connections! People laugh and joke about it all the time, but it's no joke when private matters are improperly circulated.

Here is one common way friendships within the church experience tension. You become friends with "Sue" at a church retreat, talking late into the night and discovering your common interests. You share dreams and your spiritual journey. You meet for lunch, shopping, and watching your children on the playground. Then Sue's husband has a disagreement with your husband/pastor over an incident or philosophical/theological issue that must be handled within the church. You cannot be part of the solution except through prayer; sitting down as couples to talk it out may not be appropriate if matters must be sorted by the church board. All of a sudden you realize that what seemed like a true, deep friendship, can't be continued with the same freedom you once felt. She must be loyal to her husband and you to yours. If Sue is your only friend, it may be harder for you to look at the situation objectively. This is just one of many reasons why your relationship with the Lord and your marriage need to be top priorities. If your focus has been on friendship and fellowship with one person, the crumbling of it can be devastating. Thus, wisdom and discretion are critical components of developing friendships within the church.

Whether the challenge is juggling your schedule, facing expectations, dealing with criticism, or choosing friends, retaining your footing on the balance beam of life comes from being based on the foundation of God's Word.

Action Points

- Do you know any widows of pastors? Reach out to one with a phone call or visit. When the time seems appropriate, encourage her to consider sharing the wisdom of her years with you.

- Need a respite? Contact a friend who does not live in your area; plan a "girls' getaway" from both your homes and have fun for one or two days to help you gain perspective.

Chapter 3

Excess Baggage

Calculating the Cost

"HALF THE WOMEN IN OUR SMALL NEW CHURCH,
including me, are in counseling, primarily
for family-of-origin issues. It would be interesting to find out how many ministry wives are
struggling now with painful roots of the past."

These words were written at the end of one of the
surveys returned by a minister's wife outside the United
States. Of course there is no way to find out a precise
answer to her question. But no one (including parents) is perfect, and no family, no matter how wonderful, is without
cause for working on some important family issue. Not
everyone has painful roots as far as family life is concerned,
but everyone does experience pain and is challenged to
make changes as he or she grows in Christ. When we
are married, we face those challenges in new ways.

Whatever traditions and habits we have formed
are sure to meet with new ones when we
begin to realize how many different
habits our spouse has.

Volumes have been written to sift through biblical evidence that thoughts, habits, and judgments are passed on from generation to generation.[1]

Adjustment, balance, give and take, mutual submission—all of these are part of marriage. Baggage is also part of the equation. The term sounds negative and heavy, a buzzword in psychological jargon meaning something from our past that is carried by us on our life journey.

If marriage were the only destination for the baggage, that would be reason enough to want to lose the claim check, but for couples who enter ministry, baggage carries even more significance. Because close bonds are formed in the Christian life, church members become our extended family, and we often call them brothers and sisters; thus we cannot keep the contents of our baggage a secret forever. Missionaries traveling to foreign countries sometimes request prayers that they will not have to pay for excess baggage. Unconsciously, many of us live our lives the same way, hoping and praying that we will not have to pay for the extra pounds (consequences) of past issues we have brought into our marriages. Ideally, at least for the congregation, a minister should have inspected and worked through all of his baggage during his ministerial training so that he is the model the parish wishes him to be. But if he is married, his wife may have had no formal education to prepare for ministerial marriage; unless she has had specific education or counseling to deal with issues of her past, she may carry quite a load of baggage herself.

An older man, now out of ministry, sadly told me that he had lied to his ordination committee when they asked him if his wife was with him in his desire to enter ministry. He so strongly desired to be a pastor that he sinned to get past the system. But after twenty-five difficult years, the marriage and ministry ended. He thought he could store the baggage that plagued the marriage, but it didn't work.

God's Preparation

Anyone who has dealt with the issues related to their past knows that there are times in life when we are ready to face them. The Lord prepares us through our spiritual journey, providing significant people and various educational avenues along the way. Only when we are ready can we work through them honestly and thoroughly. It is usually a very slow, painful process, but the freedom one feels after crossing a major hurdle is worth that process.

Bill and Lynne Hybels say that for couples who fail to discuss and understand each other's painful pasts, there is "always ... some kind of backlash."[2] Further, they urge couples considering marriage to spend innumerable hours talking because it "can be a rich, trust-building experience as partners learn that it is okay to be real, that there are no wounds, no secrets, no memories too embarrassing to reveal. And it can foster the oneness God had in mind for marriage as partners share an ownership of each other's past and a mutual respect for each other's journey."[3]

My Journey

The First Leg

Dealing with my baggage began as a seed in my mind during late adolescence when I knew that there was a void in my life that had been caused by the death of my father when I was four years old. He was thirty-four and was sick for only a few short days before he died. I thought I "handled" the loss well, but I knew that somewhere along the road of life I would discover just how much of a void had been caused and would learn to deal with the consequences of his absence.

As a young person, my gut wrenched when I heard God referred to as "father to the fatherless" (Ps. 68:5). I didn't realize that I had stuffed away pain, anger, and hurt that would later fall out of my baggage like dirty laundry. I shudder to express it even now, as it seems disrespectful, knowing how God often provided himself in the flesh of other people, but I must express it in order to explain the situation. I wasn't too sure about God's defense of widows either, or descriptions of God as judge, protector, defender, one who brings justice.

My mother has been a Christian since she was a teenager, always faithful in her Bible reading and church attendance, taking my sisters and me to church. I believe she looked to God to meet our needs, making a giant move away from family so we could get a Christian education. She taught me the importance of having a thankful spirit for everything done for us as a family and as individuals. I am continually surprised by God's goodness to me. But our lifestyle also had negative aspects. One that stuck with me was distrust. I don't know if my mother ever made an actual statement to this effect, but lodged in my mind was the thought that everybody was out to get widows for all they were worth; therefore, we had to live on the defensive, suspicious of everyone's motives. She was especially careful to use only reputable car repairmen so that we weren't likely to be cheated. As an adult, I realize such business decisions are wise, but being wary of people lest we fall prey to them was what settled within me. I tried to decide that I would not grow up distrusting people, but I found early in my marriage that I had failed.

I Didn't Carry All My Baggage Alone

Within a few months of my marriage to Ed in 1972, our travels as an evangelistic team ended, and Ed was working for my brother-in-law in his grave-digging business. My husband came home from work many days muddy and wet. One night when he arrived later than usual, I gave him the distinct impression that I wasn't sure I believed that he had been doing what he said he had. When he realized that I was suspicious, he was deeply shocked that I didn't trust him. As we talked about it, I was surprised, too. I was doing exactly what I had told myself not to do.

Ed determined to build my trust in him. He has been God's provision in the flesh to aid my healing process. He has never given rides to women and has never gone to lunch with them alone. He has appointments with women in the line of his secretary's vision and will not have an office door without a window. He keeps in close phone contact with me throughout the day whether he is in town or away from home. In every personal and intimate way he has worked to help me overcome this mind-set. He has never given me cause to mistrust him.

Checking the Route

I don't know what my father's relationship with God was like. I have been told that he was a Christian and that early in their ten-year marriage my parents had solid biblical teaching. I have never heard anything unkind said about him by anyone on either side of the family. But he was gone, and life went on without him.

Because I was four when my father died, I did not process emotions in the same way my six- and eight-year-old sisters did. The loss and grief occurred at different times as I began to understand it, but it wasn't until I was over forty that I located the spot where I had left my baggage. It was my last memory of my father alive. Because he had been removed, my basic concept of God was that he also was removed from me. I trusted him fully in my heart and mind, and I received assurance of forgiveness of sins at age eight and was baptized soon after that. My desire to witness to others developed, and I became well grounded in the Scriptures. But even with all that biblical knowledge and a sincere desire to know and love God, I felt an empty spot when it came to feeling the love of a father.[4]

In high school, when I sensed that friends felt sorry for me because I did not have a dad, I sniffed and retorted that I'd rather have him dead than for my parents to be divorced. I thought the quick, cold dismissal said I was handling the void in a mature way. I realized later that I had "put on layers of self-protection to cover damaged emotions . . . [to] conceal a wounded 'little girl' trying to survive."[5] I was acting out anger for his absence. I didn't realize what I was doing at the time, and I am not sure when my desire for my attitude to change occurred, but probably before I met my husband. I had been through a stormy dating relationship and had finally relinquished my list of requirements for a husband to only one item: that he love God.

As a result of my sense that something was missing because of my father's death, I determined in my innermost being that somehow I would find out what it meant to know God as Father. At the time, I knew him only as a disciplinarian; I knew that I must obey because that was the way things were. Period.

I not only heard good things about my father from both sides of the family, but was told that I was like him, both in looks and in mannerisms. I felt that, if he had lived, he and my mother would have had a good relationship, the type I wanted to have with a husband. While those concepts are based on the few facts I remember, they still continue into my fifties as anchors to my feelings. I did not realize that the first four years of my life were essential and sufficient for me to have experienced and felt my father's love. During the writing of this chapter in the early 1990s, I was able, through the help of a friend who is a professional counselor (God's provision), to identify a specific time when trust was built into my love bank: I remember Daddy bringing home a puppy in his pocket. Once I recognized that my real memories of him were full of love and of the expression of it, I was able to grieve his removal from my life and my lack of control over that. I am now able to see that while the years I had with my father were few, they were good and provided the foundation I thought was missing. I confessed my anger to God and repented of my unrealistic view of him. This opened the door of my heart for feeling the love of my heavenly Father that I missed for so long.

My Silent Journey

In my quest to know God, I read the Bible through many times, with the underlying prayer that the Holy Spirit would help me see God as he is, as I needed to know him. Not until I became urgent about it did I begin to put in writing the thoughts that helped cement the knowledge of his love for me and his readiness to restore and forgive when I stray or lag behind in development. I became brave enough to start a devotional book, a type of journal that would reveal thoughts I didn't want anyone else to know. In fact, that was the reason I hadn't used that method before, except during intense pain, such as the death of a friend. I was afraid that after I died somebody would find my journal and be shocked by my admissions and failures. I feared they would see me as a spiritual undergraduate, not the sophisticated product of a Christian higher-learning experience—and a pastor's wife at that!

Putting aside those fears because of my longing to know God, I began by underlining and writing out verses in the Bible that made mention of God's "unfailing love." That phrase appears regularly only in the New International Version. It was the key I felt I needed to unlock the old suitcases I thought were empty, and I latched onto it, writing it out and reveling in its implications. I often compared verses that contained the phrase with the Living Bible, King James Version, and the New American Standard Bible. I wanted to know every possible angle of what it could mean.

Some of the passages I recorded were Exodus 15:13; Psalm 31:16; 32:10; 36:7; Isaiah 54:10; and Hosea 10:12. Exodus and Deuteronomy list the commandments as they were given to the children of Israel. They were reminded over and over to fear, serve, love, and obey God. God is jealous but shows love to a thousand generations of those who love him and keep his commandments (Deut. 5:10; 7:9). I began to see that despite the waywardness of the Israelites, God expressed his openness that if someday they would return to worship him alone, he would be ready to restore and forgive them. He was there for me, too.

A beloved song-writing friend suggested that I write out the verses on God's unfailing love, one at a time, in each version, like this:

Psalm 36:7:

NIV: "How priceless is your unfailing love!"

TLB: "How precious is your constant love, O God!"

NASB: "How precious is Your lovingkindness, O God!"

KJV: "How excellent is thy loving-kindness, O God!"

Psalm 90:14:

NIV: "Satisfy us in the morning with your unfailing love, / that we may sing for joy and be glad all our days."

TLB: "Satisfy us in our earliest youth with your lovingkindness, giving us constant joy to the end of our lives."

NASB: "O satisfy us in the morning with Your lovingkindness, / That we may sing for joy and be glad all our days."

KJV: "Oh, satisfy us early with thy mercy, that we may rejoice and be glad all our days."

Isaiah 54:10 (read when the California earthquake struck at the beginning of the World Series, 1990):

NIV: "Though the mountains be shaken and the hills be removed, / yet my unfailing love for you will not be shaken nor my covenant of peace be removed."

TLB: "For the mountains may depart and the hills disappear, but my kindness shall not leave you. My promise of peace for you will never be broken."

NASB: "For the mountains may be removed and the hills may shake, / But My lovingkindness will not be removed from you, / And My covenant of peace will not be shaken."

Putting these and many others together in written form helped produce with the guidance of the Holy Spirit a sense of peace and rest based on knowledge that God truly is loving, not just to the whole world for the salvation of souls (John 3:16), but to me personally—all the time. He had always been a Father to me, the fatherless; I just did not recognize the breadth of his fatherly love. In recent years my trust and love for my heavenly Father has grown, particularly because of an intense time spent with him while struggling to write a Bible study about his attributes. On a new level I have realized how my old attitude must have grieved his heart. My rebelliousness in holding him at a distance must have pained him when he wanted me to feel his comforting love.

What I have discovered about God as Father carries over into ministry. He has caused me to feel a sensitivity toward single parents, and I can understand to some degree those who struggle with accepting the concept of God as their Father if they have never known the love of an earthly father. I have also discovered, however, that women who have been "Daddy's girl" may have struggles, too. If he has always been available to them and has fixed every problem they had as a young person, their concept of God may be shattered when their world falls apart and they think God should fix it like Daddy always did. No matter how we may have misconstrued our image of God, we need to be in the Word, searching and pleading with him to let us see and know him as he truly is, not blaming and judging him for specific events in our lives.

Baggage in the Parsonage

If you are harboring unresolved issues from your family of origin or in your marriage, sooner or later they will surface in ministry. I cite here three examples.

An anonymous ministry wife has called me a number of times. She is so fearful of hurting the ministry in which she and her husband are involved that she doesn't want to reveal who or where she is. My desire for her is that she and her husband will see that having a whole marriage is part of their ministry. Hiding the problems will only make the eruption more deadly when they surface. And they will surface eventually. Thankfully, I think she is making progress, and I have been able to refer her to other "safe" resources for help (see appendix).

Another example is that of someone close to me. A dear friend of mine left her husband after a few years in ministry but many years of marriage. I was devastated emotionally. Even though I was sure there were aspects of their past I didn't know, I had great confidence that they were on the path together, excited about their place in the Lord's service. For years she did not respond to my calls or letters, until I told her about this book project. Quickly she answered with an urgent message for me and for the readers: "It wasn't the ministry that hurt our marriage. If the marriage had been what it should have been, the ministry only would have enhanced it." For me to understand, she took me through a seven-page journey, beginning when she was fifteen. She urged me at the end of the letter to "tell the pastors that going to Bible school doesn't make them God." She meant that training for the ministry should not replace taking care of old, unresolved issues. She also may have meant that some men in ministry think they are above questioning and refuse to be held accountable by godly people.

The third citing involves reasons behind decisions made about our children's involvement in activities. A discussion began when my husband told a group of ministry couples that he has made every effort to attend as many of our oldest son's soccer games as possible. Ed's parents saw only Ed's last college game. His parents have been loving and godly, having served in the ministry for many years, and his widowed father is still supportive of his ministry; however, Ed missed having them present when he played sports.

One pastor after another expressed hurt, anger, and disappointment over the fact that their ministry parents had never attended, approved of, or noticed what their children's interests were. Much of our generation struggles with wanting to "be there" for our children, at times out of a payback, "in-your-face" attitude for our parents not being around to watch us unless they were pushing a favorite sport or talent they did not have the opportunity to develop early in life. A few in the group said they were not bothered that their parents were not present for activities; perhaps in that particular community, culture, or time, there was no peer pressure for the parents or children.

In defense of ministry parents of baby boomers who balked about their lives being so structured that family devotions were held regardless of conflicting children's activities, a biblical factor may be noted: God's Word does not return empty (Isa. 55:11). The men in ministry today who struggle with unresolved conflict also know and love and teach the Bible because of the foundation laid early in their lives and because of the consistent prayers of their parents. The adult children now in ministry need to deal with past hurts so that what has been tucked away will not continue to hinder their spiritual growth and so that they will not live a life of overreaction by letting the next generation do too much in conformity to the cultural norms of the day (Rom. 12:1–2).[6] We must not simply live out our lives in reaction to the way we were reared.

Baggage Claim

Some of us carry enough baggage to ruin any ministry in which we are involved. It is our responsibility to claim and handle it as if every piece is fragile, placing it gently where it belongs, sometimes at the foot of the cross. I think that far too many Christians glibly use the verse "forgetting what is behind" (Phil. 3:13) as an excuse to stuff problems into the attic of our minds, all the while trying to convince ourselves that old baggage was carried away in a dumpster. Dealing with issues that require a resolution takes time, energy, and fortitude. That is the price of handling the baggage properly.

Seek Christian professional help if you are unable to resolve your issues alone. By doing so in no way minimizes the importance of the Word of God or the Holy Spirit's work in your life; godly counsel can help you gain perspective on all sides of issues. Sometimes we need only a momentary enlightenment to say, "Aha! So that's why . . . ," and at other times we need guidance to diligently sort through years of placing in the baggage dirty objects that should be discarded through forgiveness instead of being hidden from view.

You may delay payment for excess baggage for decades, but you will pay much in interest along the way. You may lose your credit rating among Christians as well as with those who have no "ticket to eternity." Once the collection agency takes over, your plans to serve the Lord may be set aside or even shut down completely, and you will follow the path of those who have been left at the terminal or rerouted so many times that they miss the best of what was planned.

Persist on your journey even if you have been rerouted or hijacked.[7] Sheer delight and freedom from the mental weight of carrying excess baggage or from searching for and reclaiming lost contents awaits those who have the courage to pursue God, holiness, and wholeness. The reward is a complete set of coordinated luggage, a heart and mind attractively and unashamedly carried to each destination.

Wherever you are in the journey, take heart and claim the promises of God. Get a grip on biblical hope, such as that which was given to the exiled children of Israel (Jer. 29:11–13):

> "For I know the plans I have for you," declares the LORD, "plans to prosper you and not to harm you, plans to give you hope and a future. Then you will call upon me and come and pray to me, and I will listen to you. You will seek me and find me when you seek me with all your heart. I will be found by you," declares the LORD.

Action Points

- Are you ready to work on some of the "baggage" of your life? Make it your mission to ground yourself in the Word as you work through difficult relationships. Solicit your husband's prayers and support. Whether you do this work in a Bible study, counseling, or alone, remember that this hard work can *feel* lonely, but it will drive you to the arms of your Savior, and the benefits will be freeing.

- Do you feel that you have it all together because your marriage is great and your birth family functioned in a healthy manner? Ask God to reveal his heart of mercy and grace to you as he brings others not so fortunate into your life. Read books on forgiveness, boundaries, and other issues God brings to mind.

Chapter 4

First Things First
Sorting the Laundry

WHO *REALLY* COMES FIRST? YOU KNOW THE
answer; it is the cornerstone of your faith.
Oswald Chambers gives this blanket answer:
"There is only one relationship that really matters, and that is your personal relationship to your
personal Redeemer and Lord. If you maintain that at
all costs, letting everything else go, God will fulfill His
purpose through your life."[1] Because living out this principle every day is difficult, I find it helpful to read about and
discuss with others how they maintain this priority. Since I
discuss the importance of one's relationship to God
throughout this book, I am not going to deal with that
directly in this chapter. It is, however, an integral part of
each area that I will address here—namely, the ministry wife's relationships with her husband and children, and integration of family life with church
and her husband's occupational calling.
When I began to write down questions, issues, and struggles

that kept surfacing as I talked to ministry women, I realized that nearly every one of them truly wants to serve and please God but cannot decide in given situations whether to put family or ministry first. If pat answers were available for every situation, dependence on God's wisdom (James 1:5) would not be necessary.

Sorting the Laundry

Working through the responsibilities and commitments of our lives to determine who and what comes first is a little like sorting laundry: you wash whites and colors separately, but when you dress, you combine the colors with whites. In career ministry, you may try to separate items in your thought processes, but everyday living requires the combination of all aspects of life. Those who determine to keep issues separate in heart and action appear to be frustrated in more than one area of life. Let's look at some of the issues relating to family members separately, beginning with husbands.

The Whites—Your Marriage

Before we spoke the vows during our wedding ceremony, Ed and I determined that our commitment to marriage would be top priority in our lives together, second only to our personal relationship to Christ. Keeping our separate lives pure was and is essential to keeping the marriage clean. Pulling out of the marriage if times became rough was not an option. When a wife tells me that she has had thoughts of leaving her husband, or when I read a book written by ministry persons who say they have wished they could walk away from their marriage, I may understand what brought them to that point, but I cannot relate at all. I have never had such thoughts.

Even though both spouses are committed to the marriage, if you become parents, you may unconsciously allow the busyness of child rearing to let some years pass before realizing that your relationship as a couple has lost its brightness. Your focus has been on the children, their growth and activities. Couple that with ministry, and you may have a marriage in disarray![2]

Remembering our early days in Virginia, I can quickly empathize with couples beginning a work who may inadvertently fail to attend to their marriage. Ed and I were still settling into wedded bliss yet starting a church and working at a college thirty-eight miles away. I tried writing letters to my husband when I was frustrated, but they were so complicated that he did not understand the way I expressed my needs. We did not fight during those early learning years, but I had some lonely times. Now Ed has developed the ability to write wonderful letters to me, particularly if he is away from home. I can seldom take the time to respond in writing as thoughtfully as he does.

Today we look for practical ways to make moments for communication or togetherness. (This does not mean blinking as he flips through the cable channels!) I try not to schedule activities for myself on Ed's day off, so that we can plan something together; however, we do not follow that rigidly. Sometimes we only work on the budget book, but at least that is an hour of talking through important issues. Other days we run errands together, take care of household projects, take a walk in the woods; or he may play golf with friends while I do something else.

We have gone away overnight for almost every anniversary, participated in ministry retreats and conferences for many years, and have taken a few vacation trips without children. We feel that time alone contributes to a healthy marriage and ultimately to a healthy family. Good intentions of scheduling time together are not enough, because calendars have a way of filling and leaving no together time. We have to make time. When the house was full of teens, it was more convenient to have lunch together than to have evening dinner dates. Seasonal changes in life help prevent dating plans from becoming stagnant.

I am a bit concerned, however, when I hear ministry couples speaking of absolute "date nights." Ministry seldom allows for this kind of rigidity, and it isn't necessarily biblical. Paying a baby-sitter isn't always affordable, and grandparents (free baby-sitters) are not always available. For example, to say that you will never be available on Tuesday for anything that is happening in the church may leave you open for resentment if "your time" is broken by someone else's crisis. Leave room for flexibility while still making your marriage a priority.

Looking past the necessity of cultivating the marriage relationship on a regular basis right now, we need to look to the future of our marriage. It is as wise as setting money aside for house or car repairs and retirement. Many years ago an older ministry wife warned me, "You'd better be looking for something to do with your husband that you both enjoy, because someday the children will be gone, and the two of you will be left alone." She posed some questions about activities:

- Do you exercise together? (I walk; he runs.)
- What sports do you play? (He used to play soccer, tennis, and racquetball, but I gradually gave up every sport because of wanting to protect my hands to play the piano.)
- Do you bowl or skate? (These are activities we endured with young children.)
- Do you bike? (I can't sit on the seat because of several falls on ice.)
- Do you cross-country ski? (We tried, briefly.)
- Do you golf? (Now there's an idea, but it's expensive. The Lord has worked in interesting ways to make the development of this venture a limited reality, and we have found that we enjoy being outdoors together doing this, even when we play lousy. We laugh a lot, and there is no phone to answer.)

Here are a few other questions to consider:

- Do you both enjoy a certain style of music enough to attend concerts together?
- If you both love to read, is there a way to share what you read so that you are not holed up in your own quiet world?

- When the children are grown enough not to need a mother's constant attention, what ways can you minister together?
- What unfulfilled dreams can you help each other realize?
- Do you have a hobby you can develop together?
- How will you fill the hours formerly spent in driving your children to activities and watching their performances or sports? Will they be traded for hours of baby-sitting grandchildren? (I hope so to some degree!)
- What if doing ministry together, which you'd hoped for more of as your children reached adulthood, was no longer an option?

We had a few dead-end conversations about how we could spend more time together. Then Ed blew out his knee playing indoor soccer during the late 1990s and had to have surgery, which terminated his soccer days. During his recovery, I said, "I think we could enjoy taking walks or day hikes together. There are so many beautiful places to see in Michigan." He bought an encyclopedia of walking that included everything one would need to know about backpacking. He became a fanatic. Because of a camping disaster in the 1980s, I told him I would not go camping with him again until he learned more about it from a member of our church who teaches survival! Yes, we have taken some day hikes, but we also have had wonderful times with our grown children canoeing and camping. Some of those times have been with our "instructors," now friends. We've taken walks in Israel to places we never could have seen by making quick stops on a tour bus. It has changed our lives, and we love it! For years *vacation* was synonymous with clean hotels and sitting on the beach. Now we dehydrate food and filter water—for fun! The time-consuming preparation and cleanup are worthwhile for the hours we spend outdoors. Sometimes the conversations are lengthy and thought provoking. At other times we are too tired to talk, but we enjoy the time together anyway. We plan to keep on enjoying the outdoors as long as God gives us strength.

Develop your marriage in ways that will enhance your whole family life. If all of the above sounds simplistic to you because your marriage has left you feeling as if you have been through an old-fashioned wringer washing machine, keep working, trying, hoping. Many books are available for couples who desire to grow together and keep the romance sparkling. Move past your reticence caused by fear of hurting your husband's ministry; pray continuously about it; deal with important issues; read helpful books. Don't just wait and hope it will happen. Follow the example of couples you know who demonstrate loving steadfastness; find out how they have worked on their marriages. If you are unable to work on your marriage satisfactorily as a couple, seek the help of a qualified Christian counselor.

Some Colors Have Run into the Whites

I thought I had taught our children how to separate colors for the wash, but when I asked thirteen-year-old Heather for light-colored sweatshirts and towels, stating specifically (rather loudly up the staircase) not to bring green Christmas towels, she thought she heard me say *to* bring them. She also threw in a few of her brothers' white dress shirts, which I later discovered slightly green. Life gets very complicated when the colors run together. When communication breaks down, the result is a mess that is very hard to remedy, especially with the husband-wife relationship. What you think you have said clearly may not be heard or interpreted clearly, and the result is not pretty.

When I surveyed ministry women, I wanted to know how good the couples' communication was, so I asked, "If you could say anything to your husband, and if you knew that he would listen with a bent to understanding what he hears, what would you like to say to him?" Twenty-four percent of the women indicated that they have good communication with their husbands; they talk everything through and have developed trust, have worked at the marriage, have become aware of each other's weaknesses, and have become best friends. Some said, "He cares, he listens, he responds." A few among the other 75 percent provided the following answers, which give us some insight into their challenges:

- "You seem to have more time to hear others than me."
- "Sometimes I just need your undivided attention or genuine interest."
- "Talk to me; don't surprise me with your schedule."
- "Your family needs you on a more regular basis, with no tapes, books, or anything else on your mind."
- "You give your best time, listening and caring, to everyone before me."
- "Listen to me as carefully as you do your parishioners."
- "Be there for me and the kids; be interested in 'us.'"
- "We get the anger, no patience, no time when we are away [from home]. You don't want to talk. It's very frustrating. I don't have anyone. The kids have their friends to share with. Life has become too serious."
- "You love the Lord with all your heart and the church second. When do we receive some of your time?"
- "Stop fooling yourself that we have a family life. When the kids aren't in school, you either aren't home or are too strung out to interact with them."
- "When I come to you with a problem, I want you to be my husband, not my pastor. I don't want a sermon. I'm not one of your counselees. I want sympathy and understanding."

Over and over I hear women say they don't want to approach their husbands about the difficulties mentioned above because they are in the Lord's work. They are guilt-ridden for feeling upset over such issues. Consequently they suppress their anger, letting it simmer, and they ooze out periodic complaints until finally they erupt and hurl blame in all directions. Edward Bratcher assesses the situation this way:

Many ministers can be faulted for having the immature belief that if they are doing God's work, God will take care of their wives and families. There is no biblical evidence to support such a view; however, the feeling that God provides a special protective shield and/or companionship for the minister's family while he is away doing "the Lord's work" is prevalent. Such a view spells *neglect!*[3]

Yet many pastors are caught in the middle, having no intention of neglecting their families. I can see many aspects of my own family's life in the candid interviews in Stefan Ulstein's book *Pastors [Off the Record]*. When people know that their pastor sincerely loves and cares about them, they will demand more and more of his time, "catching" him at a ball game or making a quick phone call to his house because they don't want to "bother" him at the office. "Sometimes it's new people who don't know how to work the system," and older people don't want to try. The pastor feels that "the meter is always running."[4] Frequently we hear, "I know it's your day off, but...." The only way to spend quality, uninterrupted time as a couple is to leave town, but that is very hard to do when children are at home, when finances do not permit it, and when the schedule is too demanding for both home and work.[5]

Laundry Is Never Done: Keep Testing Detergents

If you have felt a desperate need to get away just to feel a sense of relief from the pressure and to be alone with your spouse for building or rebuilding your marriage, look at what could be the consequences of not taking time away from the urgent to work on the important. Women whose marriages and/or ministry were torn by painful experiences said that their husbands should have listened to them for insight, that they should have made time for the family, and that they should have considered their wives' wishes more than they did.

Ministry couples and parents would do well to listen and heed the warnings from the brokenhearted before it is too late! Begin with a simple suggestion, like a spontaneous drive along the lakeshore or out in the country—anything that will change your scenery and provide time together. More suggestions are listed in chapter 9.

My heart prays for women who feel that their husbands have put the church first. I pray that they will never give up trying new ways to refurbish their love as it was in the days of courting, and that they will not give up hope that the marriage can improve. The wife of a former minister whose clergy life had been devastated and whose marriage had revealed the need for some work as a result, told me this with joyful tears in her eyes: "I prayed that God would help me begin to see the qualities in my husband that attracted me to him when we were dating, and God is doing that!" Throughout the day she would be reminded by a simple gesture or by a smile from their son, who looks like his dad at the same age when the couple fell in love. It was an exciting confirmation that God was beginning a renewal for them.

Let's Get Perspective

How important is it to put family "first"? When I had two small children, I was invited to a Bible study in a historic stately southern mansion. The hostess was a mother of four young children; she wanted to grow as a Christian but felt lonely in a new community where few of her acquaintances were of her social standing and wealth, so she reached out to others. One statement she made has played in my mind like a broken record: "Our family is our mission field, and we dare not miss the opportunity by being too busy for our own spiritual growth and our children's spiritual education." She helped me see that no matter what our status in life, our responsibility to minister to our family is more important than looking for other ways to serve the Lord. That thought has often given me impetus to say no to opportunities that would crowd my calendar and take me away from my family. For instance, Saturday morning is usually the only day of the week that I can cook breakfast for the whole family at one time; therefore, I almost never go to Saturday women's events at church. The same is usually true for my husband and the men's ministry.

Staying at home for family time may not seem as spiritual as attending a church function, but sometimes it is more important.

A friend, whose family disintegrated while they were in ministry, asked me to tell you this: "Love your children, hold them, talk to them, play with them, do nothing with them. They will remember it as though it were printed on their hearts. But if they miss the opportunity, that, too, will be printed on their hearts."

Do we want our children to think that their world is important to us? Do we hope that when they hit the crises of life they will share their needs and hurts with us? If so, how are we communicating that to them? Children need to learn the balance between interrupting others who are talking and persisting because of an urgent need. Parents who teach their children that they are to be seen and not heard would do well to consider that the child may live that concept when dealing with temptations that may send him or her into a life of sin. We don't want to be the last to know when our children are in trouble or hurt.

When Should I Use Baby-Sitters?

When my children were young, it seemed as if I spent half my time on the phone finding baby-sitters. I often flipped through the church directory thinking, *Now who was that who said she would be glad to help me in a pinch?* The whole issue was not only time consuming, but taxing, exasperating me to the point that I felt that it was not worth the trouble of trying to leave home! When I could make the arrangements, it seemed that I was paying a lot of money for child care even though I didn't work a job for pay outside our home. I asked our accountant if I should keep track of money paid out for baby-sitters. He advised me to keep a record of what I paid for child care only when I had to attend a function because my husband is a pastor.

I pondered that instruction many times even when the issue was not baby-sitting money: How many of my activities would still be on my schedule if we were not in ministry? People invite us to banquets, concerts, fund-raisers, and other events because my husband is a pastor—either for our enjoyment, for his information, or for his endorsement of their organization. But I attend some events with or without him regardless of the fact that he is in ministry, because my involvement in the church is primarily related to the gifts and interests I would develop anyway. Since we recognize that it is physically impossible to attend every event, we weigh many of our decisions based on what is good for family timing rather than on what we feel we "should" do. Thus, I soon decided that keeping track of money paid to baby-sitters was unnecessary.

More difficult than the money issue was my desire to be available for more ministry opportunities: I am a sucker for wanting to volunteer whenever I know of a need for service. Thinking that I was doing a spiritual thing, I prayed for four years after we moved to our present pastorate that *someone* would be available to take care of my children so that I could do anything I wanted to do in ministry. After all, I knew of ministers' wives who had someone to take care of their children after church so that they could stand by their husbands and shake hands with people as they left church. But it never happened for me. We are blessed with friends who were willing for any of our young children to do whatever their family was doing at any time, but no *one* person has ever come along to do my bidding. I accept that as a spiritual lesson and the answer to a very selfish request.

For two years in the mid-1980s, my mother lived just four miles from us in Virginia. She came to our house when the children were sick so that I could play the organ for church. But when we moved to Michigan, no parent was close by. Was it right for me to ask someone to stay with my sick child while I went to church to play the piano for choir? My husband did not think so, and eventually I admitted to myself that I agreed, although it hurt my pride. I considered my responsibility to choir important, but when I stayed home and listened to the church service on the radio, I realized that very few people could discern who was playing the piano because there was a capable substitute. I learned that the choir did not need me half as much as did my family. The Lord continues to humble me by showing me that I am dispensable and that the work can and does go on without me.

It is important to take our calling and stewardship of our gifts seriously, being responsible when we cannot fulfill the obligations of a commitment. However, it is more important to be available when our child needs Mommy. Our children are gifts from God and are our mission field, and we dare not neglect ministering to their needs even though at the time it may not feel as rewarding as public service. Time with them can be used by God to mold them as well as us.

So How Do I Decide Who Comes First?

While the institution of the church was ordained by God, the husband-wife relationship was instituted long before that, followed by family relationships. The result of a person's fellowship with God will be direction to conduct matters of service within orderly biblical principles for the family. Church programs should not be the only ruling factor in the life of the ministry family, but because ministry = people = time, we need to be careful stewards of our time.

I have been asked such questions as, "How do you know when to give up or be late for a church activity to go to your son's soccer games?" "Must our teenagers attend the church my husband pastors?" "My child hates going to catechism class because of the way the church treated us when we went through difficult times; but if he doesn't go, it is noticeable to everyone, and his dad teaches the class. What should we do?" "Our church's tradition dictates that many functions coincide with school-related activities. We want our family to be an example of faithfulness to others who aren't involved; how do you 'make' your children get involved?"

Some of these questions may be answered in a twenty-minute conversation, sifting alternatives, praying for wisdom to do the right thing; others are not so easily answered. The more complex the challenge, the more parents need to sort through the issues verbally, listing pros and cons on paper, never ceasing to seek the Lord's face and search the Word for what may apply to the situation. There is safety in a multitude of counselors (see Prov. 24:6), so it may be wise to see a counselor if you are struggling with a question that is much more complex than deciding what games to attend.

Sometimes You Need a New Appliance

In February 1993 my old Maytag washer ground itself to a rubber-smelling halt (the morning I was preparing lunch for twenty-five missionaries!) and was replaced by a new one the next day. At the same time, our family struggled with a major ministry decision that demonstrated one of the most radical statements we had ever made regarding our family. This was the situation: Spring break coincided with our church's five Easter cantata performances. As in the ten performances of Festival of Lights at Christmas, Ed's main mission was to present the gospel clearly and concisely; I was to play the electric keyboard with the orchestra. We would have no time later on for vacation as a whole family, because our son Kent probably would be working in New York during the summer. Did we dare leave the church's evangelistic outreach for family vacation? We had had so much fun on spring break the year before and realized that we might not have many more opportunities for a trip together in the future. Ed discussed the situation with the church board, who gave him their blessing on whatever decision he made. We chose family, 2,500 miles of togetherness! The associate pastor took Ed's place, speaking the gospel clearly and concisely; the new assistant to the music minister "happened" to be a fine pianist who knew much more than I about the functions of the keyboard. We arrived home from vacation in time to enjoy the final performance. We had a sense of peace that we had done the right thing for our family and ministry.

A few in the church misunderstood. We just keep doing the laundry, sorting as each situation presents itself, weighing our responsibilities as parents as well as remembering our calling and commitment to ministry.

Ten years have passed since we bought the new Maytag. Sometimes the children remind us of something they enjoyed about the vacation we took at that time. Time spent with them was and is still valuable. We are not "empty nesters" yet, but we are thankful that each child (now adults and adolescent) is demonstrating a desire to walk with the Lord. Our hope for them is simply in 3 John 4: "I have no greater joy than to hear that my children are walking in the truth." We want to feel that joy for our physical children as well as our spiritual children; both require the investment of our lives into theirs. Sometimes we must change methods and machines to help accomplish the goals.

Action Points

- Frazzled because of too many activities and expectations? Plan a family getaway that forces everyone to do everything together. Make one meal a day or, at the very least, one meal a week together a priority. Connect daily with everyone in your immediate family. Let your children know that their parents are trying to strike a balance between expectations and commitments of ministry while keeping family a priority.

- Wondering what to do as your family requires less attention and time? Reevaluate your current service to the Lord. Is it time to launch into something new? In what ways could your husband benefit from your more active involvement with him?

Chapter 5

Feeling Alone
Sharing in Christ's Suffering

THE PHONE RANG, AND I HEARD THE VOICE OF A
policeman who said that if my husband, Ed,
did not appear at the police station by 7:00
P.M., officers would come in two squad cars,
handcuff him, and take him away. Our first son
was a newborn, and in that moment, as the blood
seemed to drain out of my body, I wondered if I would
even be able to care for him. I couldn't believe this was
happening to us! We were serving the Lord! My husband
was a preacher!

It was a fall day in the mid-1970s. Ed was dean of students at (then called) Liberty Baptist College. He was on
the soccer field coaching; I could not call him. And I did
not feel that I should call anyone else until he knew
what was about to happen. I felt totally alone.

A new law had been passed in Virginia but had
never been tried. It stated that if anyone suspected another person of child abuse
but did not report it, the first

party was subject to arrest and punishment. My husband had been caught in the middle of discussions of suspicion of child abuse. Although he had never seen the child, Sunday school workers who were suspicious had called him, after which he talked to the party suspected of the abuse and to doctors who had seen the child. They all knew that the problem should be reported but had not settled the question of who would be the appropriate person to call authorities. About that time the child was taken to the hospital with obvious signs of having been abused again, and someone decided that my husband should be arrested. Ed spent several hours in a jail cell with no shoelaces and no belt, sitting among drunks and other obvious offenders. The phone rang as he walked in the doorway of our home with our friend and president of the school; it was someone demanding that Ed return to the police station because they forgot to take his picture!

The case dragged through the system and was thrown out of court by a judge who said it was obvious that the wrong person had been arrested. The joy resulting from the decision did not erase the memories for us.

This book would be unrealistic if all challenging situations were mentioned in general terms; therefore, it is with reluctance but with a sense of necessity that I share moments like this when I have felt alone. My hope is that when you face difficult moments in your life, you will realize that we all face them; we just can't talk about all of them, and that can produce the feeling of aloneness.

Nearly every time I read 1 Peter 3:13–18, memories of the above incident enter my mind. No, I wasn't the one who sat in the jail handcuffed, but I was part of the situation, and I learned early in ministry that we sometimes suffer for doing good rather than evil. It is one way we can get a taste of knowing Christ and "the fellowship of sharing in his sufferings" (Phil. 3:10). Oswald Chambers put it this way: "If you are going to be used by God, He will take you through a number of experiences that are not meant for you personally at all. They are designed to make you useful in His hands, and to enable you to understand what takes place in the lives of others."[1]

My part in this incident cannot compare with the agony experienced by the abused child and the family. My life has gone on with joyful relationships between family members, while the child, now an adult, must surely have ongoing difficulties.

My heart is burdened for volunteer workers within the church; no precautions are stringent enough to protect them from being accused of damaging children emotionally or physically. Conversely, no precautions are too stringent for screening the workers for the sake of the children. Some people will look for any means, even using the church and their children, to try to make money or draw attention to themselves. When accusations are made and lawyers are brought into the situation, these difficulties cannot be talked about except with the parties involved. Even though I have no part in the process that is handled by the church board, what I do know about the situation, and what I remember about our own circumstances years ago, can be added to the list of moments when I feel alone. It is a challenge to develop my prayer life, communication with the one to whom I can divulge everything. Reading Job's arguments with his friends helps me sort through the complex situations in life that seem unfair. I am awed by his undying trust in God: "Though he slay me, yet will I hope in him" (Job 13:15).

In this chapter I deal with types of moments that trigger the feeling of aloneness, that sad feeling of desolation. We have some positive choices to make regarding how we deal with those moments, realizing that improper handling of the challenges could lead to bitterness, anger, depression, and burnout. Lonely moments should drive us to communion with the Lord whom we serve and contribute to the strengthening of communication with our mates.

Where Do I Turn?

All ministry involves being with, working with, and dealing with people in their best, worst, and growing times. Some people joke, "Ministry would be great if it weren't for people!" We constantly take risks by getting involved in people's lives. In one day we may attend both weddings and funerals, sharing the joy and laughter, frustration, anguish, and suffering of the families. All of this is emotionally draining, and in the midst of ministering, loneliness may jump us and throw us off balance. We may wonder where to turn to get our own emotions recharged. The answer is obvious, but at times last on our list: the Lord Jesus Christ, our Savior, Redeemer, Friend, and Counselor is with us, ready for us to turn to him. The weight of helping carry the burdens of others can cause us to lose sight of how to maintain equilibrium or obtain help for ourselves.

Carol Kent differentiates solitude and loneliness this way: Solitude is aloneness we choose; loneliness is suffering that comes from a lack of intimacy. Intimacy is a need met by a personal relationship with Christ. "In many moments when people disappoint us—and they will—we still have a Covenant Partner who says, 'I will never leave you nor forsake you.'"[2]

Why do many Christians feel alone, even in the midst of working with people? One reason is our human need for replenishing. The Hybels have categorized all relationships as draining, neutral, or replenishing.[3] I have heard James Dobson say numerous times on his *Focus on the Family* radio program that a large measure of the problem of loneliness among women lies in the disconnectedness of women to women in America today. Many are in the workforce where relationships demand more business than social contact; mobility and job transfers break extended family units.

Even in full-time service for the Lord, we sometimes place schedules above relationships. We get caught up at times in the self-promoting, materialistic, performance-based society in which we live. God's people are not immune to the fast-paced status-climbing complexity of our day. I know ministers who have sued coworkers for matters of perceived injustices rather than resolving conflicts biblically. This tears the unity of the body of Christ and distracts us from the real mission: being and making disciples of Christ. And it leaves behind hurting, lonely people who at one time were enthusiastic about spreading the gospel.

When People Hope You Fail

We entered the mountain town of Buena Vista, Virginia, in 1973, to begin a church. The editor of the weekly newspaper told my husband that other outsiders had tried and failed to start churches. He stated bluntly that he was sure that we would fail, too. While it was a discouraging word at the moment, Ed felt that it helped spark within him a positive attitude and a passion to succeed. The church remains today.

When you feel that you are an archery target and the community has the bows and arrows, this kind of statement can be the jolt you need to motivate you. Our youth provided at that time some of the energy to rise above the moment. It was accompanied by the determination not to let the opposition have the satisfaction of seeing us fail and by the will to fulfill God's call in spite of discouragements.

Culture Shock

Although less than 1 percent of the women I surveyed mentioned loneliness as a significant frustration in their lives, many listed factors that contribute to loneliness. They included moving, living away from relatives, and sharing their husbands with many people. I continually hear from caregivers of ministers and their families that this is a recurring theme.

Dr. Diane Langberg stated on a "Pastor to Pastor" tape produced by Focus on the Family that missionaries are prepared for culture shock while people preparing for ministry in America are not. This lack of preparation is what Marjory Foyle has in mind in writing that pastors' families are among those who experience stress when they "remain within their own countries but cross state boundaries, which often involves adapting to a new language and unfamiliar local culture despite being of the same nationality."[4] When ministry families move to a large city from a close-knit small-town setting, adjustment is difficult. The reverse is equally trying, as was the case when we moved to Buena Vista; the fishbowl was stifling. We bought our first home a few blocks from the church. I loved walking along the quaint streets but felt that I was seen and known by everyone.

The first time I sought help in Buena Vista was shortly after the formation of the church. I attended a midweek service even though I had had all my wisdom teeth pulled the day before and my jaws were packed. As the evening progressed, my pain increased, and I simply nodded to people as they left. The wife of one of the leaders sniffed and called me "stuck-up." Devastated and shocked, I tried to explain the situation but felt unsuccessful. I asked her to pray with me the next time we met, and I did my best to resolve the issue. At age twenty-four, I was not schooled in determining the issues in *her* life that caused her to lash out. I was more concerned that she not think ill of me! I did not minister to her adequately, and I received no response from a pastor's wife to whom I had looked for help. I felt alone in a strange town. Now I understand better that, as Langberg says, "acceptance is something we all want and enjoy, but it is not to be our goal. The Shepherd whom we follow was not accepted; people rejected him; he knew the feeling of aloneness."[5]

One of my most vivid memories of feeling alone is that of sitting on the front row in that church, a renovated funeral home. We had been struggling over whether to remain with the church full-time and long-term or leave it to be at the college in Lynchburg, thirty-eight miles away, where we also worked. I looked out the narrow window in front of me and saw a bird in the distance, soaring at what seemed to be an incredible height. Instantly I wanted to fly away, to escape, to do anything but remain in that little town. But I could not tell any of those dear people whom we loved. Ed and I had been instrumental in leading some of them to the Lord, and they wanted us to stay forever. We have a framed picture of us standing by that window on the day we left the church. Our faces reveal the pain we felt, even though we were sure we were doing the right thing.

That lonely feeling is intensified in situations that seem to have no hope of changing. A friend of mine felt caught in that loneliness trap even after her husband had been pastor of a church for more than fifteen years. Although she had grown up in another part of the state, she was considered an outsider. She was the only woman in the church who was a college graduate, and since there was no money to hire staff, she was compelled to help in the office and Christian school. Every day she was entwined with the ministry, taking her young children to work with her because there were no available baby-sitters. Visits to family were their only break. Eventually they left the pastorate.

If you are in a similar position, you are not alone; caregivers say that this sense of alienation is common. Why? Because, Langberg says, "many women in the congregation see you as a role and not as a person. You are not Jane or Sally; you are the pastor's wife. People often are caught between wanting you to be perfect and hoping that they will find a flaw so that they can feel more comfortable around you."[6] I had no easy solutions for my friend, who was disappointed by some outside help she sought. She learned to lean on the Lord to meet her needs and give her hope. She willingly served but lost the joy. This couple still serve the Lord in a ministry setting, but I am not sure they regained a sense of fulfillment after this difficult time. In the truest sense, we each will go through times of feeling lonely in order to learn that our Savior is always with us. We need to discipline ourselves to depend on him at all times and know that he is willing to sustain us when we feel alone.

I Can't Know or Help Everyone

At times I feel stress that comes from knowing that my own physical and emotional limitations prevent me from being part of the lives of everyone in our large church. At this point, if I ever meet every member, I will know a miracle has occurred! For a number of years, we periodically invited several dozen members to our home for an informal dessert fellowship, but the list was never-ending. Just thinking about it produces frustration, even an unnatural loneliness, because I know that when I *do* meet them, and if they act overjoyed at the rare meeting, I will want to hide at that moment. I feel slightly embarrassed that their meeting the senior pastor's wife should be such a big deal! Fortunately, in a large church, most people understand to some degree that no staff person or his or her spouse can know everyone or meet everyone's needs and that regular attendees feel a closeness to the leaders of the area in the church in which they are involved.

If your husband ministers in a small setting, you may know everyone but feel the same stress of limitations that simply cannot allow you to meet everyone's needs. Or worse, in any size congregation, you may feel stifled by a few who demand your attention and depend on you to solve their problems or approve of their actions by their feeling close to the pastor's family.

Needs of people are never all met, and wishing that I could meet those needs only compounds my frustration and expends unnecessary energy. When I feel that inadequacy surface, I give it to the Lord and ask him to help me be effective with the ones I am able to know. I was not called to meet the needs of all church members.

Having mentioned briefly the different challenges of large and small congregations, I would like to insert a caution to pastors' wives. While listening to conversations among women, I sometimes hear a competitive spirit regarding size of churches that I have also heard from their pastor-husbands. This creates a spirit of divisiveness among brothers and sisters that can only contribute to loneliness rather than comradeship. Women who think they are more involved in the lives of their members because the congregation is small are putting down sisters whose lives they simply may not understand. And if the wife of a large church's pastor has not been part of a small congregation, she may not understand the different stresses placed on her sister from a small church. We all need to guard our talk.

Being Left Out Can Feel Lonely

A nagging question once whittled its way through my mind: Would church members be our friends if my husband were not the pastor? Are they nice to us because we represent something important in their lives and it makes them feel good to do something for us? I appreciate people who include us in events they have planned, such as traditional holiday gatherings, and I am especially grateful to the ones who sensitively say that I am welcome even if my husband is away. Those questions nagged me years ago, but I no longer dwell on them, because they only create negative thoughts and feelings and can unwittingly be expressed in my actions and speech. Thinking those thoughts reveals a lack of understanding or acceptance of God's call—it is not for the purpose of making friends or climbing a social ladder.

Some pastors' wives say they have no social life and are not included in events that church members enjoy outside church activities. Although the minister's family needs help in their initiation into a new culture, some church communities are not attentive to the feelings of loneliness that accompany such a move. Remote communities are often enmeshed and refuse to accept the pastor as one of their own. Holidays can be tough, since clergy do not always have the freedom to go "home."

Frankly, some pastors could use a sensitivity lesson when they are included in social activities. Pastors' wives who have told me that their husbands want to talk incessantly about their ministry, vision, and passion are embarrassed and find that in private conversation their husbands cannot see any reason to change. While ministry talk may be appropriate at times, when the wife notices that they are not invited again socially, it may be that the parishioners would like the pastor to seem interested in *their* lives, not just his ministry.

I am periodically reminded that as far as my "role" in the church community is concerned, I am the wife of the pastor who came fifteen years ago to "their" seventy-plus-year-old church. I am the outsider, although I was born in this state and although our children have grown up thinking that this is home. It would be wrong for me to depend on church members to provide a social life for me. I need to step aside mentally and try to see the panoramic view. I am a messenger, an ambassador of the Lord, and parallel to the song that says, "This world is not my home, I'm just a-passin' through," I am not totally rooted here, even if I die while I am still a member here.

The Invisible Woman

I smile cynically when I hear Eric Clapton's song "Lonely Stranger." I realize that it has nothing to do with my own lifestyle, but the first line grabs me: "I must be invisible; no one noticed me." I think of it and pout for a few moments when I am with my husband and he is acknowledged or buttonholed for a quick conversation but I am ignored. After the person passes, I whisper to him, ". . . and ghost," and we chuckle. I could dwell on my being ignored and allow bitterness to build. Instead, I have chosen to use such experiences as teaching tools for myself and have learned to acknowledge those who are forced to overhear what I have to say to someone who is of significance to me at the moment. Ed usually interrupts the person long enough to introduce me.

Wanting to Be the Invisible Woman

The flip side of being ignored—being pointed out—can be just as devastating. A ludicrous example of this occurred one day when a woman who was introducing a talk that would have six points wondered aloud whether it should have only three. "Where is Lorna?" she asked. "I know I saw her somewhere." By then I was hiding behind the head of the woman in front of me, mumbling to those around me, "Why am *I* supposed to know? I'm a musician!" My husband's sermons often contain more than three points, and besides that, why should the pastor's wife be an authority on the structure of a talk?

This incident was mild compared to some of the deeply malicious, hurtful things said publicly to pastors' wives. It is important for us to continue to grow into maturity and realize that such statements might be made by any of us when we do not bother to think through the effect of our words on the receiver. I accept such occasions as opportunities to learn to exercise more sensitivity to others when I speak to them. Whenever possible, I lovingly confront the one whom I feel has offended me, or I try to give a good-natured word of insight if I have a level of expertise in that situation. I have since realized that although I would like to think of myself as a "normal" person, my presence is sometimes intimidating to others.

Thoughtless remarks by people may contribute to our plunging into a well of self-pity. They make unnecessary all-inclusive statements about "the pastor" or his family. When one woman remarked, "The pastor's wife is always late!" I responded with, "I'm not late yet!" I fumed for several days and chose to pity myself because the woman "picked on" me. What I wanted to say was not Christian. Nor was it Christian for me to simmer and waste energy dwelling on something I could not change.

When You Would Rather Pray Alone

Finding prayer partners can be a real challenge. After we moved to our present pastorate, I felt a lonely frustration at ladies' Bible study. In small groups arranged for prayer time, I rarely shared any requests and seldom prayed about real concerns. I did not feel comfortable talking to God about personal issues in front of women I did not know. I do not like to give people an opportunity to gossip in the name of prayer requests.

I expressed this concern to a woman named Mary with whom I felt a kindred spirit. A few weeks later she called and said that she had been thinking of starting a prayer group in her home for a small group of mothers to pray for each other's children. She planned to invite other women who were committed Christians and not gossips. The whole idea would be based on confidentiality. I could attend once, and if I didn't want to return, she would understand.

That was over fourteen years ago, and we are still meeting. Most of us have become grandparents, and our prayers have extended to grandchildren and our aging parents, along with our changing roles in relation to family members. We have supported each other in illness and in the death of family members. Only a complete memory block could keep me from praying on specific days of the week for each of these families. This is a wonderful outlet for me. I never discuss any issues related to the church unless the women are directly involved, but I do feel comfortable discussing my children. When one of my children had a crisis that could have been the top subject of church gossip, Mary was the one I called first, not just for prayer, but because I needed to talk to someone I knew had lived through and survived similar circumstances. She offered godly wisdom for how I should react and interact with the child. Mary does not expect me to behave a certain way because my husband is a pastor, and the women in my mothers' prayer group continually teach me the value of learning from others who have walked the way before me. It is an environment where I feel safe.

You, too, can develop a place of safety for sharing burdens; however, discernment and wisdom from the Lord are necessary. Being in a small church setting can magnify a challenge such as this; yet the Lord can provide ways in any situation to fulfill your desires and his directives. You may need to share your requests with a faraway friend by phone, letter, or email. Or you may begin a prayer group or join an established fellowship of ministry wives.

Dealing with Others' Sin Brings Loneliness

Few moments in our ministry life have caught us by surprise and have hurt more than when we have learned that close friends have been unfaithful to their mates. Such news triggers immediate withdrawal as we pull back and process our feelings.

We had been out of college only a couple of years when we were told that a friend whom we had admired for his talents and ministry capabilities had cheated on his wife. He and Ed had traveled together on a ministry team one summer during college, and Ed had later spoken in his church. Pleading with him to repent and to reconcile with his wife was to no avail. Both the ministry and the marriage were over. He told Ed to use him as an example any time it was appropriate to warn others; he had neglected his personal time with the Lord, drawing on his human abilities. He had laughed at sin portrayed humorously on TV until he didn't think it was so bad. And finally he began spending time with a woman in crisis under the guise of ministry.

At times when we learn of the fall of others, we should take to heart the warnings of Galatians 6:1, "Watch yourself, or you also may be tempted," and of 1 Corinthians 10:12, "Be careful. If you are thinking, 'Oh, I would never behave like that'—let this be a warning to you. For you too may fall into sin" (TLB).

I wish that I could tell you that our college friend was the only one we knew who fell morally. Other coworkers in the ministry have shocked us with their behavior, and we have stayed awake all night hurting, crying, holding one another, and praying, wishing it would go away and not be real. Sometimes we were so close to situations that we couldn't see what was happening. Later my husband recalled moments of uneasiness about his friends' actions; when confronted, they flatly denied any wrongdoing and dismissed the appearance of inappropriate behavior as unnecessary suspicion on Ed's part.

In Ezekiel 3:20 the Lord commanded the prophet to warn righteous men not to sin, for he would be accountable to God for them. We are responsible for confronting those who persist in sin. The consequences are sobering for both parties: If I fail to confront the person, God will hold me accountable; if that person falls into sin, all the good things he or she has done will not be remembered—the person will instead be remembered for his or her fall.

In a similar circumstance with a staff member, my husband lived for years with doubts about the man's honesty but could do nothing until the man was left with no choice but to confess. I knew nothing about my husband's loneliness until the man resigned. I did, however, know in my spirit that something was desperately wrong, and I prayed for years that God would do whatever needed to be done to bring that man to deal with hidden issues.

The older we get, the more we realize that sexual sins don't just "happen." They brew for years, often because of unresolved problems in the family of origin or because of character flaws that have not been dealt with at the root. No matter what the sin, it is accompanied by a perversion of the truth. When, in this life of spiritual warfare, a person chooses to sin, the waves of devastation that crash around that person tear apart the hearts of all who are in the wake. What is often called the "fall" of a leader is really only the public's "finding out" that a fall occurred sometime previously. Because it is not always appropriate for church members to know details, the feelings of loneliness are magnified for the minister and his wife (assuming she too is aware of the person's fall). Some people who do not and should not know all the facts are quick to jump to conclusions and write nasty letters to the pastor. Factions of loyalties divide the unity of the church because parishioners cannot know the whole picture, and the weight of the matter rests almost visibly on the pastor, who is, to some extent, alone. Sharing in those times is part of the "stuff" that comes with being the wife of a pastor.

Discipling Others Will Help You Leave Loneliness Behind

One strong desire in my Christian walk has been to develop the area of discipleship. I was first motivated in this area during the summer of 1966 when I worked with a missions outreach team who held five-day Bible clubs and conducted house-to-house visitation in Lahaina, Maui, Hawaii. I ached for the young people who trusted the Lord, because there was no immediate follow-up. Knowing that their homes were steeped in traditional Eastern religions, I felt that part of my responsibility was never fulfilled. But as a seventeen-year-old high school student on a short missions trip, there was nothing I could do about it.

My desire to live out my faith in a genuine way continued to grow, largely because of my personal commitment to the Bible. Even though I could not always tangibly see that I was growing spiritually, I knew that staying in the Word was vital to keeping my life free from sin (Ps. 119:9, 11).

After Ed and I were married, he met with groups of men or individuals for accountability and discipleship, but my involvement with women seldom reached below the surface. Other than working with college piano students who wished to use their talent in the Lord's work, I ministered very little. During our fourteen and a half years of working for Jerry Falwell, I was afraid of getting into discussions with neighbors about what they thought of Falwell's organization (they usually held strong opinions—either positive or negative), so I seldom found out where they stood spiritually.

A breakthrough on my road to becoming a discipler came when we moved to West Michigan and decided to place our children in public school. Becoming involved in the children's schools was natural for me, and during the course of several years, I established a friendship with the mother of my daughter's friend. She was a new Christian and asked me to disciple her. Of course, I said yes, but inside I panicked. We had discussed many doctrines and biblical issues, but I had no books with which to begin a formal study. I called a friend who is a fervent discipler. Although Carole did not in any way "put me down" for asking for help, I wondered whether I was the only pastor's wife who had not actively engaged in discipleship studies!

Carole gladly gave me all the Navigators[7] materials I needed to get started with the new Christian. The materials helped confirm in my mind that I knew what needed to be taught and that I had the right foundation through the Word. Now I finally had the means to put my knowledge to work. Since then I have facilitated many other Bible studies. Perhaps the years of waiting were necessary preparation for the journey. Ed and I have also met together with couples for discipleship. Seeing new believers grow in the Lord is one of the greatest joys of ministry.

Some Tips for Dealing with Loneliness

If you have struggled with feelings of loneliness throughout your life, the ministry may not be the cause but may contribute to these feelings. Biblical counseling may be needed. But here are some tips for dealing with loneliness on your own.

1. Need to be replenished? See chapter 6 for ideas that will pick you up.

2. Sensing that people hope you fail? Place your complete hope and trust in God. Focus on glorifying Christ and maintaining the spirit of servanthood that he exemplified. Whatever the outcome of the darts, you will know you followed the leading of the Lord.

3. Suffering from culture shock? Spending time with the senior adults in your church community will help you more than any other way to learn the history and expectations of the church. Ask them about important cultural aspects of the community that can help you understand your situation and where you fit in.

4. Feeling trapped or left out? Invite some other ministry wives to lunch in your home or meet at a restaurant to form new relationships with a common ground. Renew old friendships. Develop a plan for inviting church members into your home.

5. Filled with self-pity? Plunge yourself into the Word of God and read Ruth Myers's *31 Days of Praise*.[8]

6. Need to develop an area of your life but feel embarrassed because of expectations you think others have of you? Talk it over with your husband, choose a prayer partner, then take the step when the time is right.

7. Need someone to listen? Make use of resources listed in the appendix. Services are available for people in ministry. Talk through issues and gain perspective from objective outsiders.[9]

8. At the end of your rope? Bathe every facet of your life in prayer, and experience the surrounding love of Christ. In time you may view the "deep incision [of loneliness as] an inexhaustible source of beauty and self-understanding."[10] Even if your circumstances do not change, you will. Remember that at times when you feel you are all alone, you are not: "Never will I leave you; never will I forsake you" (Heb. 13:5).

Chapter 6

Personal Stuff
Taking Care of Me

IF YOU GASPED WHEN YOU READ THE CHAPTER title—I know, it sounds "worldly." It smacks of the present generation of self-centered rights seekers and self-improvement fanatics. Not to worry. Read on.

Henry Cloud and John Townsend suggest that one should not "confuse this self-absorption [to the exclusion of others' needs] with a God-given sense of taking responsibility for one's own needs first so that one is able to love others . . . without moving into a crisis ourselves."[1] They cite Philippians 2:4, which states the need for balancing our own interests with those of others.

One woman whose husband has now retired from ministry gave me this advice: "Take care of yourself physically, mentally, and spiritually. Often in ministry we are so consumed with the mechanics of the ministry and so tuned into others' needs that we strongly neglect our own needs, not even realizing that we have them!"

For the person who is involved with ministry, accepting responsibility for one's physical and mental health is as essential as spiritual growth. Practicing the daily routines of taking care of one's body, mind, and spiritual life requires discipline. I feel a sense of balance in every area of my life when I am consistent in my daily walk with the Lord, eat healthy foods and drink a lot of water, and exercise. Mentally and emotionally, I feel more capable of handling stress when the physical and spiritual are functioning properly. But it takes work; when I am inconsistent, I must recommit and start fresh.

Putting the First Thing First

No single activity is more important than spending time in the Word of God, unless it is the prayer time in which you beseech God to activate his Word in your life.

When I was young I learned passages of Scripture for family devotions and to earn my way to Scripture Memory Camp. I attended Bob Jones Academy and University, where I was required to take a Bible course every semester from 1961 through 1971. Many Bible and education classes required Scripture memory. Those Scriptures imprinted in my mind are the basis for everyday living and are also the ultimate weapon for spiritual warfare. Music also played an important part in my Scripture memorization. I learned dozens of portions of Scripture through music in high school, college, and church choirs. For many years as I have read the Bible, I have not only underlined but drawn a treble clef sign in the margin of verses I cannot help but sing as I read.

Recently I realized I had a problem that had been brewing for many years. I lied to myself, saying that I "couldn't" memorize Scripture very well out of any of the newer translations, since I had memorized so much from the King James Version when I was young. As an adult I would write out verses or passages, carry them around, read them over and over, but rarely fully commit them to memory, excusing myself because I "couldn't" memorize them. One day I started a Bible study with two friends and decided to seriously commit the coordinating verses to memory. I took the little printed cards with me as I walked for exercise, and I asked God to help me internalize and apply those verses to my life. During one of those walks, I realized that I had plastered my mind with lies about not memorizing. That was a humiliating thought, convicting me that I could read newer translations because they were written in today's language for my understanding but say to myself and others that I couldn't retain the words! I realized for the first time how that must grieve God's heart, and I wept in repentance of the wasted years of not knowing more of his Word.

I also realized that one of the lies I had told myself was that I knew a large portion of God's Word, yet there was so much more that I didn't yet know! How brazen and sinful I had been for too long! The freedom of repentance and beginning to learn again has been a sweet gift that I treasure. Now that the Bible study is over, I periodically add verses or passages to the card pouch, looking forward to those walks with the Lord when his Word is actually speaking to my heart. The life, power, and cleansing that comes from memorizing and meditating on the Word is like rebirth!

Reading through the whole Bible has been a lifetime habit. During my young adult years, I felt inept as a Bible student because I didn't take time to "do" studies, although I continued to read through the Bible, knowing that the Holy Spirit would teach me basic concepts about God and his dealings with his children. As a mother of three young children, the battle for time made a study hour difficult—actually, more like nonexistent. I felt that if I had only a short quiet time, it should be spent in the Word alone, not in reading what others said about it.

I looked at my spiritual life as lesser than other pastors' wives who were Bible teachers. They seemed to have plenty of time for study. I often heard myself telling people what I had convinced myself—that I was trained to be a piano teacher but felt no call or gift to teach the Bible, and that I would continue learning day by day, little by little, to be who Christ was working on me to be. That was about all I could handle—that is, until I felt a seed of desire growing within me to learn more about how to study the Bible and teach others how to study. I sensed that there was a need, not only in the church, but among ministry wives, to be trained to study the Word.

Several women whose husbands are in full-time ministry confessed that they skip the historical, chronological, and genealogical parts of the Old Testament because those portions do not meet their needs. I have a different view: I do not always know what my needs are and therefore feel that I must be open to being ministered to by *all* parts of God's Word, not just the ones I think I understand or that apply to my needs at the moment. Otherwise I set myself up for taking portions of Scripture out of context to meet my perceived need. I am not saying that one should not pour over the Psalms, for instance, in times of great distress. But I am saying that openness to the teaching of the Holy Spirit while reading any portion of Scripture can be surprisingly delightful, heart-piercing, or convicting, either when I least expect it or at times when I yearn for it.

For example, I fixed my thoughts on a phrase when I read in 2 Chronicles 25 that Amaziah "did what was right in the eyes of the LORD, *but not wholeheartedly*" (v. 2, italics mine). When Amaziah's teenage son, Uzziah, became king, Uzziah was instructed "in the fear of God. As long as he sought the LORD, God gave him success.... But after Uzziah became powerful, his pride led to his downfall. He was unfaithful to the LORD his God" (26:5, 16). I do not want to miss those passages that serve as warnings to me as a parent. I realize that my actions and attitudes will affect my children. Plodding through what may seem like difficult or boring sections of the Bible is worth the effort.

My Bible reading plans change; I vary them simply because I tend to get into a rut and need a fresh approach to reading. I have used many Bible reading plans and a variety of translations and paraphrases. At times I take no notes and simply check off the chapter number as it is read. At other times I mark a passage, meditate on a phrase, and write my thoughts in a prayer book or journal.

My Bible study methods change as well, depending on the purpose of the study. I enjoy word studies and topical studies but longed for years to know the content of the Bible better in order to be able to find passages more easily. A few years ago a friend taught me how to study passages inductively, focusing on the text. This was not the first time I had practiced inductive studying, but now I felt compelled to do it until I really knew the text better. After some practice sessions, I begged my friend to teach me how to teach others. I became excited as I developed my own overhead transparencies and study guides. My excitement spilled out as I told my friends; then as word got out, people gathered for several hours to let me practice teaching with them! Another friend worked through several books of the Bible with me. I devoured *Living by the Book* by Howard and William Hendricks (Moody Press, 1991) and practiced some of their suggested methods. The Lord then opened a door to teach the Single-Parent Fellowship at our church for a semester. I not only had a heart of love and compassion for them and their needs, but enjoyed meeting with them every week, watching them learn from the study of the Word.

I do not practice this study method all the time, and I have no aspirations to become a full-time Bible teacher, but I am so thankful that I have made another step toward knowing God's Word better. I do, however, feel a responsibility to teach whenever the doors of opportunity open for me.

If you did not grow up in a home in which God's Word was important, do not chide yourself for being "behind" in your growth. Remember that God accepted and loved us even though we were sinners; and no matter how old you were when you bowed at the foot of the cross, you are now on the right path. It is not too late to put the Bible first on your agenda.

Scheduling a daily time for Bible reading will help you be consistent. When my children were on different school schedules, I made time between "shifts." Now that I have only one child at home, I have fewer excuses. I have been working outside the home part time for several years and have found that if I make the time, I don't have to waste time making excuses! Practically speaking as well as scripturally, spending time in the Word in the morning helps me start the day on the right footing. When I feel robbed of that time or choose to busy myself with morning chores, I may develop an attitude problem that takes the spiritual footings right out from under me. In recent years I have been able to enjoy many evenings working on my Bible study or reading the Word, something I used to tell myself I "couldn't" do because of the busyness of caring for young children and the exhaustion after they went to bed that "prevented" me from feeling like studying. This thought was realistic at times, but at other times I used it as an excuse, or worse, as a lie to myself, as if thinking this way would absolve me of responsibility or at least guilt. It didn't.

If you do not have the freedom to choose a morning time for Bible reading because of your family schedule, you must creatively make time alone. A ministry wife told me that since her daughter and grandchild now live in the parsonage, she has no quiet time and no privacy. She and her husband are working with the daughter on guidelines and boundaries for the sake of everyone's sanity. This woman says that she needs at least fifteen minutes a day to talk to her husband, but she needs one and a half hours alone. Because she is the grandchild's chief caregiver during the day, time alone is never available. Adjusting to the loss of hopes and dreams has helped her deal with the frustrations of their situation; new hopes for the future keep her working on these issues daily. A loving support group of ministry wives has listened and watched her grow through this difficult time in the family's life.

I take comfort in knowing that God cares and understands when my heart longs desperately to be still and know him, but some days I cannot seem to find that quiet time. My mother-in-law, a dear prayer warrior and pastor's wife, assured me that as my family grew older I would have more time to spend in prayer and Bible reading. She is in heaven now, and I am enjoying these precious times she told me I would experience. If this strikes a chord in your heart, cling to the hope until it becomes a reality.

Every woman who completed my survey said that she has a personal, developing relationship with Christ. I was encouraged that for most of them, it was a priority; for those who admitted being in a "low time" spiritually, they anticipated growth and change in the future. I am burdened, however, for pastors' wives who do not know the Lord, and I pray that with the growing number of ministries for pastors' wives, some women who seek help through those resources will come to the knowledge of the truth.

Caring for My Body

There was a time when I feared that I might make exercise and eating habits so important that my body would become my idol. When I began writing this book in the 1990s, I feared that I would forever take on the shape of the driver's seat of the car or of the computer chair! Now, finally living without either fear, I realize that seasons of life shift the amount of time we spend for different activities. I know what I can do physically and what I like to do. Deciding where and when to do it regularly is not difficult. Doing it consistently is. And to start again after my routine has been shattered for a few weeks or months is harder.

If you have taken care of everyone else in your family but have neglected your own body, you should begin with a physical examination. Mammograms, pap smears, cholesterol checks, and bone-density tests may seem expensive if you are short on money, but early detection can save years of grief. Regular exercise and preventive care are only sensible. If we want to put Romans 12:1–2 into practice in our lives—that is, offering our bodies as living sacrifices, holy and pleasing to God, it is going to take work to make them holy and pleasing! The connection with our spiritual lives is strong: it is an act of worship (v. 1). As a result of these efforts, we live out the fruit of the Spirit, part of which is self-control. And only you can take control of yourself.

I was shocked from a spiritual standpoint into the reality of my responsibility for taking care of my body. A friend challenged me *not* to buy the book *Your Body, His Temple* unless I could handle a lot of guilt.[2] Of course I bought it. Because the author was a runner, and since I cannot run for exercise, I decided not to finish reading the book. Instead, I set out on a quest to discover what the Bible has to say about food, gluttony, self-control, and self-discipline in ways that could be applied to food. I was left without excuse. Nearly two years later I decided to finish the book. I took the author's challenges to practice stringent discipline in areas of my own personal struggle. I had joked for years about being a chocoholic, but after reading the book, I had to find out if I really was one. By abstaining from chocolate, I learned that I was not addicted to it but enjoyed excessively the taste of something that is not good for me. It blatantly was an area of my life in which I needed self-control.

My struggle with weight began in 1983 after a fall on ice, limiting my activity but not my appetite. Since then I have acquired a significant amount of information for making intelligent, rational, disciplined decisions about food and exercise, but I find that it takes a radical challenge for me to put the needed changes in motion. Actually, as I am writing this revision, I have learned new ways to alleviate discomfort I thought I would always have to live with and have begun a conditioning program to strengthen weak areas of my body. My point? We must not give up or quit learning; we should keep working toward better stewardship of the vessel God gave us.

If you need a biblical incentive, think about this: In 1 Corinthians 6:15-20, a passage teaching about sexual purity, Paul makes it clear that Christ and I are to be one in spirit, that my body is a home for the Holy Spirit, who was given to me by God. Having been bought with the precious blood of Christ my Savior, I cannot honor him when my body is misused. It is responsible and reasonable to deduce that I should not only "flee from sexual immorality," but also from other temptations that would hinder my body, the home of the Holy Spirit, from bringing glory to

Jesus' name. Do I bring shame to the cause of Christ because I am so undisciplined that the dwelling place of my Comforter, Teacher, and Guide is overgrown, unkempt, and unmanageable because of neglect or willful disobedience? Do I use the busy-work of the ministry or motherhood as my excuse? When the Holy Spirit shows me an area of weakness, I am accountable to act obediently. Remaining consistent is the battle between a willing spirit and a weak body (see Matt. 26:41).

No one else will take the reins and do this work for me; and no one else is responsible for me except me. We all know that the nagging of another person does not get the job done. Two outcomes are likely if we ignore our responsibility: others will not see us as responsible managers of the property God has given us, and our body may suffer irreparable damage. We nullify our witness of God's grace in our lives if our daily spiritual walk does not mold us physically.

One ministry friend who struggles with a serious weight problem reminded me that many of us Christians have a long list of don'ts: We don't drink, we don't smoke, we don't dance, we don't, don't, don't. What do we do? We eat—for fellowship. And we don't say no when we have had enough.

One writer put it this way, "I had better pay attention to this physical body God has given me! It is literally my 'vehicle' which enables me to go and serve God. If it breaks down, due to my own lack of responsibly caring for what God has entrusted to me, then I may find myself sitting on the sidelines when I'd really rather be on the field in the midst of the game."[3] A chiropractor told me about ten years ago that he sees more pastors' wives as patients than any other group of people. His theory was that pastors' wives don't give enough credence to the physical effects of stress on the body.

Resources abound for becoming knowledgeable about what to eat and how to exercise. Some sources are confusing, but that should not stop us from trying to do the right thing. Common sense tells us to eat moderately, but we need to do more—shun additives, refined sugars and flours, caffeine, nutrition-free foods, and hydrogenated and partially hydrogenated oils. There are many harmful substances in cardboard boxes that contain what we should not call "food," and we should educate ourselves. Common sense tells us that we should move our bodies for exercise, but it is often easier just to be busy than to discipline ourselves to work out. My husband and I decided to make an investment in our health by becoming active members of a health club. At times we wondered if we were squandering money in a "yuppie" club, but no longer.

These health considerations became of utmost importance when Ed found out he has a motor-neuron disease. We were praying for wisdom and were bombarded with suggestions, tapes, books on nutritional and alternative healing helps, not to mention devotionals and dozens of books on prayer and healing. Ed had already read the medical textbook, several nutritional books, information by other people with motor-neuron diseases, and more. In the midst of the changes we were making, my mind was spinning when I read, "Wisdom is supreme; therefore get wisdom. Though it cost all you have, get understanding" (Prov. 4:7). I felt immediately that we were on the right path, knowing that if we sought wisdom, God would give it to us. It would cost us time in learning as well as money, and we would have to give up some foods we had enjoyed in exchange for much healthier foods. There were some magnetic wellness products we wanted but didn't have money to buy, and we asked God to provide for those items if that was what he wanted us to have; in every case, the money came when the bill was due. By placing a high value on doing the right thing to help Ed build his immunities, the whole family benefits! Believe it or not, he has been "healthier" since he found out he has the disease than he had been for many years! By partnering in his care, my own body is being cared for better than it ever has been.

Taking Care of the Rest of Me

Few decisions changed my life as dramatically as the one I made to quit teaching piano when our daughter was three. This was several years before our second son was born, and I was privileged to be able to stay at home with the children through their growing years. Because we had been introduced to natural vitamins and earth-friendly household products through network marketing during our first year of marriage, I kept a small business going in my home, telling people about the products as I had opportunities. I never tried to build a big business, but I made enough money to supply products our family used. As the years have progressed, so has my desire to learn about more nutritional and wellness products that will benefit our health. Not many people in our church know that I have been a distributor of various products through the years, simply because I do not want them to be afraid when they see me coming toward them that I am going to try to sell them something! I want to walk this journey with integrity. I talk to people in our church about my business only if the subject comes up in conversation and I feel it is the right time. We have been distressed over tactics of businesspeople who use the church directory to help their business grow, and I have tried to work discreetly so that my husband will not be embarrassed by my business practices.

In the back of my mind I have held on to the idea that if I should ever need to earn a living, this would be the way for me to do it. This way of thinking was part of my life, because when my father died at age thirty-four, my mother was already a nurse and had a way of supporting herself and three daughters. I have known a number of pastors' wives who had no skills or interests outside their churches, and when their husbands died suddenly, they had no clue what to do next. I did not want to live out of fear that something might happen to my husband, nor did I want to be completely unprepared if he could no longer work to provide for our family. Besides, networking is something I love, both in ministry as well as business; learning more about healthy products is something I like to do; and meeting people through this avenue has offered me new friendships and even some opportunities to share the gospel.

Realizing that not everyone has the choice not to work outside the home (we all agree that homemaking is work), I talked to a working friend whose husband has been a pastor for nearly thirty years. I wanted to know whether she ever felt at wit's end and how she dealt with not being able to quit. She admitted that it would be nicer not to have to work, and she misses the one-on-one ministry opportunities she had during the days when she was an "at-home mom." She also misses going to the church through the week to see if there is anything that needs to be done that no one else wants to do; she is able to continue her major involvement in the church. But she sees a bright side of the issue; a whole new area of ministry has developed with women in the church who work. Their hearts have opened to her because they know she empathizes with their struggles and frustrations related to time commitments. There is a kindred spirit between them that she never knew was missing. She sees her job only as a paycheck, not a career, with the goal of someday being able to quit—perhaps when their daughters have finished college. This friend has said many times over the years that no matter how difficult our situation may be, there are parishioners in far worse circumstances, and we are responsible to God for the attitude we choose to let settle in our hearts. Rather than assuming that being forced to work outside the home will hinder our ministry, we can strive to see where it will strengthen our ministry.

About 12 percent of the women surveyed are employed by their churches, one-third of them working part time. My husband has always felt that if I were employed by a church he pastored, the possibilities for tension and misunderstanding among staff or members could be greater than if I were a volunteer. Because I felt that anyone else doing a job worthy of pay *would* be paid, my attitude toward his reasoning was at times slightly resentful, although outwardly I was submissive and complaint. However, as I have learned to trust Ed's judgment and leadership through the years, I realized, after several specific instances of having to turn down potential paying jobs in the church, that he was right, and I was thankful for God's protection. As a volunteer I see ministry from a different perspective than a paid staff member.[4]

Forty-two percent of survey respondents work outside the home; a few others work in their homes. This survey was taken about ten years ago, and I would venture to say that a similar survey taken today would probably indicate that more women have in-home businesses. Their reasons for working vary from paying back college or seminary loans, earning college tuition for children, needing their own identity, doing it because they love their work, wanting to keep licensure for professions, and supplementing their husbands' incomes. Some feel that their work is ministry apart from the church.

I had a "nearly empty nester over-fifty crisis" and had a desire to work outside the home. Several years ago the owners of my favorite coffee shop had been looking for an "older lady" to work part time during school days. I had often thought that it would be a fun place to work, making bagel sandwiches, grinding coffee, making specialty coffee drinks, helping customers find kitchen gadgets, or making gift baskets. But I never told anyone I would like to work there, mainly because I had been so consumed with organization of music, rehearsals, and particularly performances at the busiest time of the year, Christmas. Now that I had "retired" from playing the piano regularly, I had more time and would be available when this shop was busiest—Christmas season. I assumed that my husband would think I had totally lost my mental faculties and that the owner, knowing what my husband did for a living, would think the same thing! With or without the faculties, it works, and I have enjoyed being in a place where very few customers know or care anything about the rest of my life. I don't have to prepare anything for the job, and I don't have to take work home with me. I can pray silently for coworkers or customers at any moment, and I sometimes have opportunities to discreetly speak encouraging or life-giving words to people.

This job opened just a few months before I really needed it as a refuge. By the time Ed knew that something potentially serious was developing in his body, I was glad I had a job that kept me from my usual trips to the church, dropping off used clothes at the

Family Life Center, stopping to chat in Women's Ministry, handling forms in the business office, copying for classes or the missions committee—just to mention some of what I often do. Several months of uncertainty passed for us, and then we waited a few more weeks after knowing his diagnosis was "probable ALS" before he was ready to make the news public. We were trying to process our own emotions as facts rolled in, and we needed time to talk to our family, key staff, and close friends. Ed announced the news to the congregation during each of the three services on the first Sunday of December 2001; after that we had to deal with people's responses as they tried to process their own emotions. I was truly glad to have my job and not be darting in and out of church offices and not playing the piano regularly where I would have been in view of many people. I appreciated everyone's concern and prayers (and still do), but it was difficult to explain everything over and over again. In response to my explanation at work of what was going on medically, one coworker said something that helped me regroup: "But it might *not* be [ALS], right?" I responded affirmatively with my lip still trembling, but I carried that thought, and it helped me keep from looking further ahead than the moment. All the "what ifs" would get me nowhere except distraught and defeated spiritually. God is still helping us through each day as we learn to depend on his grace and strength.

Having this job has helped me balance my life emotionally. There are many ways in which all pastors' wives can care for their emotional and mental health, some of which were indicated on the survey. These related to ways in which they actively engage in fellowship (retreats or getaways), education, or enlightenment.

Getting Away

When asked how many had attended retreats for fellowship with other ministry wives, 27 percent responded affirmatively; five women indicated that they attend church retreats for women, not specifically for ministry wives. While I did not ask for reasons for attending or not attending retreats, I can surmise from statements I have heard from ministry women that the availability of information and funds is a factor. Because the pastor's wife is often not a staff member, the governing body does not usually allocate money for her participation in such events.

Retreats with a spouse are sometimes for staff fellowship only. Many of the 33 percent who said they had attended a retreat with a spouse said they had done this only once or infrequently. When asked if they were aware of specific caregivers whose sole ministry is to ministers and their spouses, half of those who responded said no, which may be the reason why more do not attend retreats with their spouses.

Approximately one-fourth attend denominational or fellowship conventions annually or more frequently. Some with small children feel that the effort to leave home is not worth it and prefer taking time alone with their husbands if they are going to make child-care arrangements. A few attend a yearly wives' day during these conventions; some would like opportunities to meet with other pastors' wives; still others do not find the meetings to be beneficial. In recent years I have learned that some denominational meetings for pastors' wives focus on fund-raisers for youth and educational needs within their churches, which, while worthy causes, may be contributing factors to the ambivalence of women to attend.

"Do you and your husband ever take trips alone?" I asked. Forty percent said they get away as a couple, although one of those stated, "Rarely," and another, "Once in twenty years." Thirty percent take trips with their husbands for occupational enrichment, and 23 percent travel with their husbands when their husbands have speaking engagements. In response to the next question, "Would you make any changes in this area?" the answers varied. Reasons mentioned most by the nearly 10 percent who would make changes were small children, lack of time off allowed by the church, or insufficient finances.

Enrichment

A few of those questioned have taken advantage of their denomination's continuing education programs; a few others are in graduate study, including seminary and counseling. More have enrolled in seminars for leadership training, such as Stephen's Ministry and Evangelism Explosion. Some are involved in Precept Bible Studies and Bible Study Fellowship. Many are avid readers. Although only one survey respondent mentioned Christian radio, I believe that listening with discernment can be uplifting, even preparational for ministry in everyday life. Topics discussed on informational, current events, and call-in talk shows can be beneficial in sensitizing us to the needs of others and spur us on to spiritual growth.

I asked survey respondents to list the periodicals they most enjoyed. The top Christian periodicals mentioned on the survey, not including denominational publications, were *Leadership, Joyful Woman, Marriage Partnership, Just Between Us, Christianity Today, Discipleship Journal, Today's Christian Woman, Focus on the Family,* and *Moody Monthly.*

I am enrolled in a lay counseling certificate program (Caring for People God's Way), available on video and audiocassette, produced by the American Association of Christian Counselors. It has been offered through our church for several years. This is broadening my understanding of the complexities of people's lives and giving me more tools and resources for referrals when I talk to people whose needs are far greater than I am qualified to help. (See appendix for further information.)

Counseling

Marital counseling, further education, self-esteem needs, and ministry-related personal issues ranked even in importance with the need for having enough money for medical and dental care. Sadly, two women cited issues that caused me to wish they had not remained anonymous. Their answers sent me to praying earnestly for intervening help: One woman said there was "strife in the home no one knows about; my husband needs help for his anger," and another family needed financial counseling—"We go deeper and deeper in debt." Several felt the need to go outside their church for spiritual growth in order to be learners, not leaders. Sadly, we are seeing and hearing about serious issues like this, not only in the church, but among ministry couples.

Among women whose husbands are no longer pastors, the need most often stated was for marital and personal counseling. The prohibiting factor: "Who was there to talk to? My husband was 'the' senior pastor." One woman offered this hope: "Several years ago we spent six months in counseling—expensive, but the best thing we could have done. I had to work through concern about what people would think, but because my husband was open, it paved the way for others to seek needed help." Becoming vulnerable is one of the scariest parts of ministry; but as one wife who had been married to a pastor for forty-five years said, "Because we were transparent and open with our people about personal failures, their expectations are not unrealistic." Another former pastor's wife about the same age told us that being vulnerable was not "in" when their children were young. She feels that his silence on personal or family struggles placed immeasurable stress on them.

Tending to My Friendships

My friend Margaret who challenged me to read *Your Body, His Temple* was a high school friend, and the incident occurred at our twentieth class reunion. Several years later she put a plan in motion for five longtime friends, all from different states, to spend four days and three nights talking almost nonstop at a bed and breakfast place in Amish country, Ohio. Some of the conversations included very old unfinished business (several of us have been friends since junior high). To hear each one's spiritual journey was an answer to one of my frequent prayers. We laughed and laughed and even made spectacles of ourselves at a photo booth in a mall. We have retreated together three times since that first reunion and are now all connected by email, planning another reunion.

Connections to my past help me step away mentally from the pressures of today. When I sense that acquaintances in church are superficial because of a misunderstanding of "what" the pastor's wife is or simply because of time limitations, I know that it is not because I am a superficial person. Friendships take a long time to develop, so keeping the good ones is worth the effort.

My sisters are my friends, and being nurses, they are often the answer to my emergency questions. We live hundreds of miles apart but keep the phone lines and email hot and the postal system in business.

I do have some close friends in our present church, but as one ministry wife writes, "'Close friends' does not mean exclusive friends."[5] Among the survey respondents who feel frustration in developing friendships because of the occupational hazards, some are resigned to the way things are and are guarded. More than three-fourths have friends outside the church (including unsaved friends, family, and other pastors' wives). About the same number have at least one close friend in the church, although most who said yes to the question did so with qualified hesitancy. Spouses should be each other's closest confidantes, but many husbands seem to understand that women need female friends.

The need for discretion cannot be emphasized enough when your friends are also members of the church your spouse pastors. If you as the pastor's wife are aware of situations being handled by the leadership, such as church discipline or staff problems, you should not be discussing them with friends, even if you feel the need to vent frustration.

Years ago I had to tell one of my friends that I could not go to lunch with her because I might talk about things I should discuss only with the people involved. I was trying to sort through my emotions after a staff resignation; disappointment, hurt, and anger were all too close to the surface for me to have a good time over lunch with a friend. I assured her that my saying no had nothing to do with her personally but was owing to my not trusting myself at that point. As the pastor's wife I was privy to confidential information, but I was not part of the process of handling the problem; therefore, I had to take the precaution of not talking, not only for the sake of the person who resigned, but so that I would not sin by saying the wrong things in the wrong way in my weak moments.

Granted, every Christian needs to guard her or his tongue in the same type of situation, but being the pastor's wife compounds the need because of the potential for causing divisiveness. Rather than my talking to friends, the Lord provided several warm fall days and some time for me to paint a fence and transplant bulbs. Time alone was well spent thinking and praying in silence.

Your closest friendships do not need to be with other staff wives. While it is important to have good staff relationships, "there is no unwritten law requiring you to be 'best friends' with fellow staff wives."[6] In our situation, staff wives get together periodically for lunch or for an evening, but we are never all together, because most of the women work and live far apart. But the bridges have been built so that any who wish to pursue personal friendships may do so.

One word of caution may be helpful: When a married male staff member contemplates resigning, the senior pastor's wife may experience awkwardness toward that staff member's wife. Whatever the reasons for the person's leaving, it may be inappropriate for the pastor's wife to discuss the situation. This may be true even for staff who have considered one another good friends and who have no ill feelings toward one another. Once a decision is made and officially public, the wives may be freer to talk openly, but until then there may be an awkward time that can be handled only with prayer and silence.

Someday I Want to . . .

One of the rewarding ways of taking care of oneself is to begin to work on that list of things you have always wanted to do. Years ago my list read something like this:

- Learn to read a chord chart.
- Take calligraphy lessons.

- Learn the technical aspects of proofreading.
- Finish picking the four layers of paint off two wicker rockers and a table I have been working on for years.

I was well into pursuing all these things when I became sidetracked with this book—and writing was what I *really* wanted to do! Since then I have studied or done work on each item in the list.

- I took contemporary improvisation piano lessons for several years, which helped me read chord charts better when playing with orchestra or band at church.
- My calligraphy instructor told me that I had very good eye-hand coordination. This encouraged me to use paint techniques in my home, having fun I never would have dared before!
- After picking paint off wicker rockers, I painted one and the table, then gave the other to our son and daughter-in-law, who prefer the weathered look.
- Every time I study the technicalities of proofreading, I become involved in a new writing project. Is there a message in this for me?

I'm not working on a specific list of things to do at the moment, because I am enjoying being a grandmother. Every time I push Lucy in the stroller or watch her demonstrate a new stage of development, I'm thankful God let me live long enough to enjoy this nearly indescribable gift of watching my child's child grow. She is a new opportunity for frequent and lifelong prayers. I love hearing her mother talk to her and seeing her father enjoy her. Because of Ed's diagnosis, Lucy's entrance to the family has brought a welcome break in what was, at least for a few months, an air of anxiety and the focus of most conversations.

In the preceding pages I have given some examples from my own life of educational and enriching pursuits. Developing my interests and gifts has varied through the years. In surveying pastors' wives, I learned that not all respondents were sure of their gifts. Not all currently use their gifts due to their season of life or to having to fulfill other needs at this time (particularly in a new or small work). Some who have been in ministry for decades said they have helped in nearly every area of church work at some time. Discovering and developing your strengths, gifts, and interests is a wonderful way of taking care of yourself. And putting them to use is fulfilling.

What If My Husband Won't Take Care of Himself?

The following statements were made by ministry wives who care deeply about their husbands. I wonder if, in their conversations with their husbands, they are not being heard.

- "Slow down; pace yourself."
- "Enjoy life; relax; find a hobby."
- "Spend more time with friends."
- "You cannot go on much longer like this."
- "Take better care of yourself."
- "Exercise; don't watch so much TV."
- "God is building the church and doesn't need you to wear yourself out; keep your rest in God!"
- "Be a marathon runner, not a sprinter!"

Perhaps your taking care of yourself will spur your husband to take care of his personal needs. Look for innovative ways to spend time together to work through some of these areas of concern. But in the end, he must conclude on his own that taking care of himself is his responsibility. More about this subject will be covered in another chapter.

Want to Say Something?

Part of taking care of yourself is using opportunities you have to pass on your passion or vision, your knowledge or expertise, to others. Because everyone may not have an avenue in ministry life, I wanted to give women who completed my survey the opportunity to say something to other ministry women. Here is a compilation of the ideas mentioned most:

- "Know yourself; be yourself; develop your unique you!"
- "Be your spouse's wife, never just the pastor's wife—no role-playing."
- "Take care of your own well-being; don't wait for your husband to do it for you."
- "Keep a healthy balance; it is OK to take time for yourself and for development in every area of your life; pursue excellence."
- "Have *fun* being a minister's wife; enjoy being who God made you to be."
- "Be honest and transparent."
- "Keep your heart right; keep short accounts; be willing to suffer."
- "Play to an audience of One."
- And one final word: "Don't have a key to anything."

Action Points

- Write a list of ways your body could benefit in five to ten years by making healthy changes. Start this week by making appointments or by joining a support group to bolster your commitment.

- Do something *totally* relaxing to slough off the demands of ministry and thereby strengthen your body's ability to heal or ward off illness.

- Write your list of "desires," then take one step to make it happen. Take a community education class to develop a hidden talent.

Chapter 7

Mutual Submission
Partnering in Godliness

SUBMISSION: SOME PEOPLE THINK THE WORD
means, "Do what he says; let him walk all
over you; be a doormat." When two young
people are madly in love, they can't imagine
that the future could hold a battle of wills, the win-
ner lording over the groveling loser. But that is what
often happens when the couple has been led to believe
that submit means "He rules She."[1]

Actually, submission means to humble or lower oneself—
which goes against the grain of humans; and total submission to God and mutual submission to each other is essential for balance in a marriage. Since Adam and Eve acted
with a spirit of independence as well as disobedience,
human relationships have been fractured by a need that
can be met only through the restoring grace of God
and sacrifice of Christ on the cross. Harmony in
marriage is achieved by mutual consent,
with the husband mirroring Christ's
example of servanthood,

being the primary initiator of love, sensitivity, provision, and spiritual concern for the family. The wife responds to his initiative by submitting to Christ and to her husband.[2]

I am thankful for the grace and patience of God on my behalf as I continue to learn and grow in this area of my life. Several years ago, I was introduced to *Five Aspects of Woman,* a Bible study written by Barbara Mouser.[3] It is a biblical theology of the created nature of femininity and deals with every major passage in the Bible on this subject. It is a way of seeing who God is, who man and woman are in their basic nature, and how they relate to each other. It is not a "to do" list or a how-to-be-a-better-woman study. God created man to picture Christ, and woman to picture the church. As a student the first year, and then a facilitator/teacher of the lessons the second and now third year, I have settled within my heart and mind the angst I had often felt about the differences in our roles. Even though I cannot claim to have settled issues that theologians will forever debate in the complimentarian and egalitarian camps, my spirit is calmed because I understand better the value and importance of woman and her role.[4]

Total submission to God is the key. Even though we may have given our whole lives—soul, body, spirit, plans, everything—to God in our youth, it is the little daily things in life, not just the big decisions, that demand submission. Submitting to what God intends for us to be or to do for him is central to living out our faith. But until recent years, I did not realize the full extent of God's created intent for my life.

Submission has a lot to do with trust. As we learn more of Christ's love, acceptance, and forgiveness, allowing them to weave through the pattern of our lives, we can rest in his total trustworthiness. Trusting in or submitting to God's ability to work things according to his will, even without our knowledge of the reasons, will help equip us to submit to others as well. Trust must be built and earned for a couple to practice mutual submission in marriage.

As a couple, Ed and I live in harmony when we are dependent on God, practicing interdependence on each other, not independence or codependence. One way my husband demonstrated his belief in mutual submission was by suggesting that before we were married we have a triangle imprinted on each of our wedding bands. It signified that we stood on equal footing under God. I recognize that we were both created in God's image, and that while Ed holds the responsibility for our marriage, we work together as a team. No matter how we define "mutual," I see him as the head of our home, and I choose to follow his leadership, which is the picture of the bride of Christ (the church) following the head of the church, who is Christ. We used to joke a lot about my having trouble with submission, but in my heart I knew it was not a joke—I had a problem with it, and only the Holy Spirit teaching me through the study of the Word helped me settle my problem.

Does Submit Mean "Give In"?

Ed and I spent many hours talking through the deepest issues of our lives before we were married, and that set a precedent for working through issues after we were married. We have disagreed and talked through our differences, but we have never screamed at each other. I have pouted a few times or become silent for a *short* time to keep from crying when my side of an issue did not "win" or I felt unheard, but those times have seldom occurred or lingered unresolved. Neither of us would "win" anything by intentionally putting down the other person. Recognizing our personality differences has helped us bypass potential spats. And although we have different habits (I don't always close cupboard doors; he drapes his ties on the closet doorknobs instead of the tie rack), they are not worth fighting over. Yes, we have been short with one another on occasion, but we do not let those times get blown out of proportion.

Ed often "gives in" over issues that are essentially unimportant, but he does not give in over issues he feels very strongly about, which I respect since he bears responsibility for our family. Once he had a gut feeling about a potentially detrimental work "opportunity" for me; I submitted to him by saying no to it and eventually understood why with utter gratefulness. On other occasions I have wanted Ed to make decisions or act more quickly, but his wisdom to wait often gave the situation time to work itself out. It takes time to learn to respect each other's ways and trust each other's intuitions. To us, "giving in" means settling the best way possible for the best interest of all parties involved. Gloating over a "win" has no part in mutual submission.

What Is Mutual Submission *Not?*

Early in marriage, part of me "mutually submitted" with a grudge because of what I imagined our roles should entail. I figured if a woman had a husband, he should take care of certain things—like changing the oil in my car. I failed to see the practicality of taking care of the car I drove all the time.

In 1977 we bought a 1971 Volvo. It was a plain—no extras—but very good car, with few miles for its age, in fine condition. Most of the time I was its sole driver, and periodically Ed would remind me to check the oil (the oil light and gas gauge did not work and were unfixable). In my mind I would say, "I'll do it later or manipulate Ed into taking this responsibility."

I taught Brenda, a college student living with us, how to drive the Volvo. One day she called to say the car had quit. The car was dead—so dead that we had to have it shoved onto a trailer because it could not be towed. But it wasn't Brenda's fault; it was mine. There wasn't a drop of oil in it. I had killed it. My "I'm sorry, dear" to Ed sounded pretty empty for such a costly blunder.

Did Ed yell at me and tell me that I was stupid and irresponsible, then send me out to get a job to pay for another car? No, he didn't have to; I had learned my lesson. It is only logical that I make the time to maintain the vehicle I drive. It is far easier for me to take it in for servicing than for my husband to make time for my car as well as his own.

We can draw a lesson on submission from 1 Samuel 15:22–23, where we read about Samuel's deliverance of God's judgment on

Saul for not obeying his command to completely destroy the Amalekites. The phrase so commonly quoted is "To obey is better than sacrifice, and to heed is better than the fat of rams," but the words that follow strike me: "for rebellion is like the sin of divination, and arrogance like the evil of idolatry." Is not the lack of submission rebellion of the heart and, even more so, arrogance? If it is like the evil of idolatry, that means that in my own arrogance and selfish desire I am actually worshiping myself and, perhaps, like Saul, blaming others for my partial obedience. He convinced himself that he had not done wrong, and he justified himself by using sinful plunder to sacrifice to God. Like Amaziah (see chapter 6), he did not obey wholeheartedly. Could rebellion and arrogance be causing the epidemic breakup of clergy marriages? They certainly are contributors.

As an older woman rereading my own words, I must add an aside. I have learned that what some women call "disagreements" that call for submission actually mean that their husbands physically back them against a wall to make a point to get their way. Any abuse, including this type of forced submission, does not reflect Christ's love for the church, which husbands are to mirror. Abuse is addressed in chapter 11.

Sharing the Load

Mutual submission also entails mutual sharing of tasks. Rigidly categorizing tasks in "his" and "her" columns is not always wise. Ruth Tucker cites the dilemma of Catherine Marshall when her husband, Peter, died. He, being the "head of the home" took care of "important" issues while she did the cooking and cleaning. Upon his sudden death, she could not handle financial matters and was not used to making such decisions.[5]

Taking a lesson from my mother's life, my main motive for obtaining a college education was to have a money-earning tool should I be left the sole breadwinner. (As mentioned earlier, my mother was a nurse before she married and was able to provide for us children after my father died.) But when I married, I unwittingly wanted to transfer all responsibility to my husband so that I would not have to do everything as Mother had done (like having the oil changed).

Ed did not want to be bothered with writing checks, paying bills, or doing the bank statement, so I "submitted" to doing these assignments. He has always carried the weight of responsibility for the decisive word on buying houses and cars; and setting up his retirement and salary packages are his business decisions. We decided early in our marriage to base our standard of living on his salary, whether or not I worked. But Ed has never liked taking care of paperwork details. I tried to talk my way out of that duty after a college friend spoke in our infant church and attempted to prove in his message (biblical reference long-since forgotten) that it is the husband's responsibility to take care of all business matters. A few months later a pastor friend in a neighboring mountain village died suddenly, and his wife was not prepared to make decisions. The shock of his death would have been great enough, but she knew nothing about their financial situation or how to keep a checkbook, and it took her a few years to learn to run her household smoothly. At that point I backed off and took on the task for our family, but I still felt some tension in the matter.

A friend helped Ed and me develop a budget, but only on the condition that we work on it together weekly. He insisted on this as a matter of principle and would not even talk about it until we agreed. It is one of the best things we have ever done. It has been the brunt of some family jokes, and the children have often wondered when it will work so well that we will have unlimited recreational spending money! I still write the checks and balance the checkbook, but I do not feel the same pressures, because Ed now participates and we talk through issues thoroughly. In no way does it compare to my keeping him informed of where the money went! He does the math in the budget book, but I could manage available money if he could not, based on the principles we have learned for saving and spending and giving.

Perhaps we underestimate the potential for confusion of our minds when swept into the tornado of a crisis. Whether we live alone or have a spouse, it is in our best interest that none of us has sole knowledge or power of essential papers under the disguise of misinformed authority. Working together lightens any load.

Survival Techniques

Having discussed a few issues regarding spousal roles, personal responsibility, and money management, we will now turn to other issues for which we need to have survival techniques ready. Endurance is not sufficient. Since ministry couples are not exempt from Satan's fiery darts, they need to protect, tend, and fortify their marriages against stress, and even be prepared for a veritable earthquake.

Communication about every aspect of life is the key to preventing potential marital quakes. Some of the most settled, contented women who completed my surveys have confidence in who they are and what their place is in life when they know they can say anything to their husbands. More than being in love, a stable marital relationship requires a knowledge and acceptance of the other person and a respect for the other's opinion and character that deepens through the years.[6]

Let's Talk about Moving

Moving is one of the most difficult stresses for ministry wives. Dahl and Joyce Seckinger, who have trained ministry couples for many years, have observed that part of the stress comes in the husband's failure to realize how difficult a move is for his wife. The way a man prepares for a change in jobs is quite different from that of his wife, who is usually concerned about details that may seem incidental to her husband. During a session for ministry couples at a retreat, I learned from the Seckingers the importance of the couple's knowledge of one another, particularly if moving is painful for the wife. Even when the move is anticipated with joy, it is not easy.

Although our family has made relatively few major ministry moves, the time spent talking before each decision has been significant. We agreed on one thing that has shaped ensuing moves. Shortly after we started the church in Buena Vista, we bought our first home a few blocks away. Ed felt that no matter how hard it was to buy the first home, once we did it, we would always be able to buy another one. He did not ever want to live in a parsonage after growing up in one, knowing how insecure it made his family feel.

Not everyone living in a parsonage feels insecure. About two-thirds of my survey respondents own their own homes; some had lived in parsonages, too, and found pros and cons for both. The most positive responses about living in a parsonage cited the cost of maintenance being borne by the church or, when church and parsonage were close together, the family's needing only one car. The greatest frustrations cited were having no equity in housing or having difficulty getting money approved by the church for repairs or redecorating. One woman who struggled for years with the desire to own a home stated that God was helping her become content; she could now see the place where she is living as temporal, not as important as it had seemed in earlier years. Those of us who feel settled in our own homes would do well to have the same attitude.

When we bought our second home in Lynchburg, we did not move "up." We decided to live within the means of Ed's income, even though I was working full time, reasoning that if we started a family and I decided to quit work or found that I could not work, we would be able to maintain what we had. Later, when we needed more space, we were able to handle the change financially without depending on a second salary.

In every move there are several factors to consider. In 1986 we were weighing ministry possibilities in Grand Rapids and New York, two very different cities and types of ministries. We talked about every area of our lives and of our children's lives that we could think of and then watched the Lord unfold the opportunities in his time. He led us to Grand Rapids.

Talk to Me—Often

Frequent communication can be a vital survival technique for ministry marriages. Daily telephone calls between home and Ed's office, truck, or hotel room, if he's away, are at times only momentary. We might not need to say much more than, "Just wanted to know how you're doing. . . . What's on the schedule for tonight?" "What did you have for lunch?" "What's for dinner?" (I try not to make him eat the same meal twice in a day!), and always, "I love you." When we are weighing all sides of an issue related to one of our children, we might discuss several times a day how we are going to handle the situation, especially if I need to give an answer to a child shortly after school. Constant communication prevents or helps halt children's attempts to manipulate their parents, and it is one of the best ways for children to learn how much their parents love them as well as love and respect each other.

I Believe in You . . .

Knowing your mate and feeling a deep-rooted trust in your love anchors you for the moment when he tells you someone has maligned his character. If his integrity or morality is questioned, your intuition brings an instantaneous reaction to support and defend him, to let him know you believe in him.

We were both glad that trust was already in place over ten years ago. Ed called me from the church to say that "Sandra" had come to see him in his office. (I remembered her: she was the one who had told him a few weeks before that neither he nor I spoke to her often enough. However, I had met her at a women's ministry function, and I had called her by name every time we passed in the nursery hallway since then.) Ed continued: "She said that she is in love with me. She says that I have been watching her when I preach as well as at other times when she is in the building, and she thinks I have feelings for her. I assured her that I don't love her and that she couldn't love me because she doesn't know me."

We were both thankful that, just a few weeks prior to that awful meeting, we had participated in a ministry retreat that prepared Ed to respond to the woman's statements. Dr. Sidney Draayer, director of Paraklesis Ministries, teaches a session called "The Minister and the Opposite Sex." The important tool Sid gave Ed through that session was how to handle transference, defined by the dictionary as "the redirection of feelings and desires and especially of those unconsciously retained from childhood toward a new object."[7] In ministry, transference occurs sometimes when (as in this case) a woman looks at the pastor unrealistically, putting him on a pedestal, thinking he is able to solve every problem and meet her needs, and letting her emotions magnify those thoughts disproportionately. Sandra let herself think that Ed was taking part in her thought process by giving her attention.

After he and I talked, Ed called the chairman of our church board and then Sid. That night the chairman met with Ed and the couple at the church. Sandra's husband expressed his commitment to make the marriage work and confirmed that he did not feel that Ed had a part in the matter. The board offered us unconditional support and offered the other couple help to obtain counseling. We thought the matter was over, but the repercussions lingered on.

The board's involvement calmed me through that difficult time. But foremost is the fact that I have never had any cause to mistrust my husband; therefore, it was easy to take his word that he had no part in the situation in question. In fact, I did not even consider otherwise.

Because there was a significant period of time when Ed fully realized that his reputation was totally out of his control, we both spent a lot of time in prayer together and alone that the truth would be known. We could not control what the woman said or what people believed, so we had to trust God to resolve the issue.

Moments of misery occurred for both of us: Ed felt distracted when he was preaching, because he was afraid that if he focused on any one person too long, that person might misinterpret his feelings, thoughts, or intentions. If he did spot the woman and her husband during a sermon, he had to consciously look elsewhere. We lived in the same community, crossing paths almost daily at school and at the grocery store. It is unnatural for me to be unfriendly, but in this case, I felt that I could not be chatty.

Several years later Ed received a loving letter from a family member of the woman. The family had endured pain for years because of her behavior and in more than one church. He thanked Ed for the way he handled the situation and for the personal integrity he demonstrated. At no time was my husband's character in question as far as they were concerned. What a relief to receive such a confirmation!

It is not uncommon for wives of ministers to feel intuitively that another woman has unhealthy feelings for the pastor. If he is unaware of another woman's manipulation to spend time near him, the wife may feel as if only an act of Congress can convince him that she is not imagining the situation. Often it isn't until someone else in the church makes the same observation and mentions it to the pastor that he realizes his wife is right.

Having talked to pastors' wives who have lived through having other women vie for their husbands' attention, we have agreed that we should not cast aside our uneasy feelings but should gently urge our husbands to observe and deal with the problem. One older ministry wife told me that "red flags" seen by the wife should be considered a gift of intuition and should be taken seriously by the couple. If the husband has been warned by his intuitive wife, he can take precautions to avoid any questionable confrontation or "accidental" meeting that might ruin his reputation. A youthful looking ministry wife of forty-five years gives this advice: "Be interesting and sharp, especially in appearance. Your husband is in contact very often with women who are on their best behavior and appearance. They would like your husband's attention." Another former wife of a pastor sends this urgent message: "Attend to your personal relationship to your husband. If he is hesitant or unresponsive *fight* for it!" Tragically, her marriage has ended. She feared the reactions of others due to the expectations of her role and the position of her husband and waited too long to get help.

Give Us a Break

Taking a break is a well-proven survival technique, but mutual submission is essential to making the survival work. Those who pastor small churches seem to especially be in a high-stress category, and husband and wife must work together for ways to relieve that stress. In many cases the church cannot afford to pay the pastor adequately and gives him very little time off. One pastor's wife told me that they had been in ministry nearly thirty-five years, and her husband still gets only two vacation Sundays plus time off for a yearly convention. Although it was humiliating for him, he recently asked the church for financial help to attend the convention; the board was happy to give it. Perhaps because the pastor had not mentioned the need before, the board had not appeared to have thought of helping him in this way. A wife's support can encourage a husband to be honest and bold with the board about a genuine need.

One ministry wife wrote on her survey that "when the stressors of marriage can be attributed to ministry, our sexual life suffers and we make an effort to get out of town alone, not on business, but to put new life into dry bones."

Leslie Flynn, who pastored the same church for forty years, learned to combine business with pleasure after his children were old enough for his wife to travel with him to denominational meetings. He would schedule an extra day or two to go sightseeing in the area. He says:

> A congregation should not expect its pastor to be continually profound week after week, year after year, without periods of extended holidays. No pastor should feel guilty about a long vacation. Look at it this way: The 60 hours a week a minister works in eight months equals the same amount of time as a forty-hour-a-week worker in twelve months. If the minister works four months more each year than most employees, it would seem that he is entitled to at least one month's vacation.[8]

Further, he explains that "pauses from intensive periods of hard work will refresh, reduce oversensitivity, fill us with gratitude, renew us for our daily work, and enable us to make our most telling strokes. In other words—help us to survive."[9]

Like the Flynns, when our children were young, vacations were always a time to visit family: either to Florida to visit my mother and her husband, or to New Jersey, and later upstate New York, to visit my husband's parents. These vacations were stress producing for us even though we wanted to see our parents and wished our children could spend more time with their grandparents.

One year we decided that we needed to go somewhere away from family, so we rented a house in Myrtle Beach, South Carolina, with two other families. With Ed trying to recover from pneumonia and just returning from the funeral of a young friend in Pennsylvania, the vacation was what we needed to make a complete change of pace and be refreshed.

The Kids Are Growing Up without You

I was visiting with a group of pastors' wives one day when one lamented: "He's out doing the Lord's work nearly every night and doesn't even know that his children are growing up without him. I guess I just have to learn to accept it."

"No!" I balked. "He needs to see the whole picture, and you must talk to him to help him see it *now,* before the kids grow up." Wives who avoid confrontation on this issue because they are afraid of overstepping the "boundaries" of submission are in error.

If a man burns out and loses his family, someone else will step into the pulpit and the work will go on. For that matter, the work goes on fine now when a pastor takes a week or two off. He needs more than a vacation once a year; he needs some segment of each week off. And if he cannot make those decisions to do it by himself, his board and/or friends and his wife owe him an avenue of accountability (even though he is responsible to take care of himself, just as his wife is).

If as a ministry family you don't take time off, you will grow resentful and envious of people in your congregation and of other ministry families who do enjoy vacation time. And most likely you will develop a spiritual martyr complex. If you are protesting as you read this that you don't have enough money for a vacation, try these suggestions offered by pastors' wives:

- "My husband gives me any money he receives from weddings and funerals; I save it for special family times."
- "All birthday and special-event money is collected and used for getaways."
- "We take our own food and visit anything that's free."
- "We take day trips and come back home at night."

Linda Riley, who started Called Together Ministries for ministry wives, suggests making use of *The Tightwad Gazette* for stretching your resources.[10] You may be innovative at making money, but if you are not, try adding a column to your weekly budget for vacation money.

Excuses for not taking time off go against Jesus' mandate to the disciples to take a break, to rest away from the people who were "coming and going" (Mark 6:31). Since resting is a biblical command, we need to be creative enough to make it happen. The pastor and his wife who are in regular, mutually submissive communication in heart and purpose will strive to figure out ways to remove themselves from their location to rest and rejuvenate, and forever memories will be created for the family.

I Want a Husband, Not a Pastor

While many women I surveyed are proud of their husband's ministry, some have expressed the need to be given sympathy and understanding during difficult times, rather than to be preached a sermon. Several women would like their husbands to hear this: "When I am upset, depressed, jealous, or angry, don't point out that those feelings may be wrong. I already know that. I am not one of your counselees." They want to be wives, not pastors' wives who should have it all together.

A husband's response to his wife's expression of her feelings may come from his belief that because he knows all the right Scriptures, he can "fix" the situation by telling her how she should feel, or by saying, "You shouldn't let it bother you." Sometimes he's just tired of hearing everyone else's problems and doesn't want to hear another one at home. Or maybe he doesn't know how else to react. Maybe he can't mentally get out of the pulpit long enough to sit and say, "I hear what you're saying. If you want help working through it, let's talk."

If the wife simply wants to cry and work it out alone, she needs to communicate that. She wants her minister husband to be real, not to play the role of someone with all the answers. If he personally stuffs away his anger over his own problems by quoting verses, he will do the same for her. He may forget that even counselees do not automatically process and practice information they are given.

If you are reading this and saying, "That's us!" you would do well to assure your husband that you are not glibly dismissing scriptural principles, but you need someone to listen as you go through the process of resolving the problem. Knowing that other pastors' wives have not only survived, but worked through these problems, helps us determine to keep working on the challenges of marriage. (See appendix for resources.)

We Are Your Parishioners, Too

A pastor leaps to answer a phone call when he has promised to build a train set with a child who needs his attention. Perhaps he has not learned to practice the difference between responding to a life and death crisis and encouraging one who can talk later to wait until office hours. He does not want to disappoint someone who calls on impulse or to offend that person by listening briefly over the phone, offering a prayer, and suggesting that he or she call the office for an appointment. Sometimes the person on the other end of the line would actually benefit from knowing the pastor has a life outside the office and that there is a more appropriate time to talk. Allowing calls to go on an answering machine during meals and Sunday afternoon naps is a good way to protect family times from interruption.

As essential as balance between family needs and ministry needs is, it is often hard to attain. Children will grow up and miss times with their dad if he always puts others first; however, they need to be sensitive to the fact that ministry is often dictated by the crises of the moment, and in those times, Dad—and sometimes Mom—must pay attention to those who are in dire need. These crises can become important teaching times for parents to explain the joys and sorrows and realities of ministry.

One of my mentors in recent years has often stated that children of ministers should not be protected from everything that goes on. The children need to know that some people hurt and therefore need the pastor's attention; that some are not perfect and so tear down the reputation or the work and disappoint the pastor; that the children themselves can be included to pray for families in need. (Discretion is a key: Don't betray confidences.)

Jim and Sally Conway offer this thought:[11] Pastors who say their children are at a disadvantage growing up in the parsonage have not taught the children realities of life—that life is painful and stressful, or that we don't have enough money for some of the things we would like to do. However, our attitude while teaching these concepts plays a big part in later life. By showing them the many positives (for instance, having people from all over the world in our home gives us cultural education one can't get in a classroom) and incorporating the attitude of helping others in ministry can help ward off the negative attitudes that often surface when the children realize nobody is perfect.

My friend who is so adamant about this incorporation of the family into ministry has proof that it worked for her family. Their son is a pastor with a thriving work, one daughter is a pastor's wife, another teaches in a Christian school, and another is active in lay ministry. They all love the Lord and each other and try to live out their faith in their communities. Their parents have faithfully lived out biblical mutual submission to God and each other.

Heavy circumstances in ministry life can be endured so much more easily when ministry spouses are at peace in their relationship. Bonding and intimacy grow as old accounts are settled and short accounts are kept. Knowing that your mate finds great pleasure in the relationship keeps tightening the knot through the storms of life.

Action Points

- Do you bristle and feel tense, angry, or defensive when you hear the words *submit* or *submission?* Begin a study of the Scriptures to learn God's intent for you as a woman no matter what your station in life. Try to refrain from holding on to old feelings or beliefs that may not be biblically based.

- Ask God to open doors of influence with other women who have not had foundational teaching regarding submission to God and to others.

Chapter 8

Enough Is Enough
Setting Boundaries

"SARA" AND I HAD BECOME FRIENDS—SORT OF.
At least she kept saying to me and to others
that we were friends. She was very interested
in asking questions about me and my family,
but it was usually because she was trying to keep
me from focusing on her problems, which were the
real topic of every conversation. I tried to help her in
different ways—encouraging her to get involved in a
small group at ladies' Bible study, leading her in a private
Bible study, praying with and for her, and listening to her,
often when I was preparing supper. But after several years,
I felt that we were at an impasse. She sweetly ignored suggestions I made for change in her life, particularly if
those changes involved giving up blatant sin, but she
continued to berate those closest to her. I told her
that she needed professional help and that I
could no longer listen to her talk about
her situation. Besides, my husband
is pastor of all her family

members, and I didn't want them to feel that they could not talk to their pastor if they so desired just because they perceived us to be "buddies."

Fortunately, Sara recognized what I had said as the truth and did see a counselor. During the next few years we greeted each other cordially but pursued no friendship. "Let's get together" always meant that she wanted to tell me her problems. I promised to pray for her but offered no more active ministry.

Situations like Sara's make it difficult to determine the difference between ministry relationships and true friendships. Several women wrote on their surveys that they have developed health problems because of their inability to separate themselves from others' problems. The test seems to be whether we are "nurtured by our friends" (based on the principle of being able to comfort others as we have been comforted, 2 Cor. 1:4).[1] If the major reason for the time spent together is *because* you are a minister or the minister's wife who is being called upon for help, retaining personal boundaries may be one way in which you can keep the door open to help the person. In Sara's case I felt too drained from her problems to feel comfortable sharing any of my own struggles. The chemistry was not right for a two-sided friendship.

One pastor's wife asked, "Is it a good thing to have boundaries, or are they going to be hurtful?" The dictionary states that a boundary fixes a limit. That is all. Knowing the difference between hurt and harm is beneficial. Establishing a boundary may *hurt* a person, but if her feelings are considered, it will not *harm* her.[2] The person most often hurt in the long run is one who fails to have boundaries. Whether a boundary is a good thing and whether it is perceived as hurtful by others depends on the way it is presented or received.

Because establishing boundaries seems like a risky thing to do, many people wait until they are stretched to their limits before they establish boundaries. It is similar to what was discussed in chapter 6; sometimes we wait until a doctor tells us we are killing ourselves by improper eating habits and lack of exercise before we limit the bad and discipline the good we do for our bodies.

I established early in the book that we as pastors' wives have dedicated our lives to the service of the Lord and that there are many times when what we have planned for ourselves is superseded by the needs of others. However, there is a time to set limits on the invasion of our person, for we may be overwhelmed by the needs of others who may wipe their feet on ministry people who inadvertently appear to be doormats. Ecclesiastes 3:1, 5–7 bears this out:

> *There is a time for everything,*
> *and a season for every activity under heaven:*
>
> *... a time to embrace and a time to refrain,*
> *a time to search and a time to give up,*
> *a time to keep and a time to throw away,*
> *a time to tear and a time to mend,*
> *a time to be silent and a time to speak....*

The boundaries addressed in this chapter are everyday issues that are pertinent to how our lives are entwined with the ministry. Bill and Lynne Hybels sorted through this in their own lives and ministry. They stated that having boundaries involves taking mature responsibility for

> our attitudes, our feelings, our behaviors, our thoughts, our abilities, our wants, our choices, our limits, and our negative assertions. People with strong boundaries ... discover their abilities, ... acknowledge their wants, ... know their limits and live within them, ... confidently make negative assertions. They know who they are, and they aren't afraid to let other people know who they are. People with weak boundaries aren't quite so sure who they are. They are not in touch with their separateness from others ... don't understand where their responsibility for others ends and their responsibility for themselves begins. They often end up being more affected by what others feel, think, want, or choose, than what they feel, think, want, or choose themselves.[3]

Henry Cloud and John Townsend assert that "appropriate boundaries actually increase our ability to care about others."[4] The "distinction between *selfishness* and *stewardship*" is similar to the argument for taking care of oneself, as discussed in chapter 6.[5]

Some of my boundaries, instead of being like our dog's chain-link fence—made of steel and set in cement—are like the picket fences around our garden. When I first put them up and painted them, they were quite sturdy. Later I had to remove a few rotten boards. Finally, I determined that one fence really wasn't useful, and I removed it altogether. Boundaries sometimes need adjustments or are no longer necessary for a new season of life.

Let us look at some common areas that require boundaries in order to protect ministry families from overexposure.

The Phone

Telephones are necessary conveniences that offer many options, and we try not to let them rule our lives. We have two phone lines—one unlisted and one listed. Because mainly family, church board, staff, and a few friends have the unlisted number, we answer it promptly when we are at home—it's usually an important call. I sometimes have to make a mad dash if I am home alone talking on one line when the other line rings! The listed phone is often in use in the evenings, especially when family members are checking email at different times; however, people who need to reach us can at least leave a message on our voice mail. Call waiting is an added convenience but should be used with care and caution; it can also be very annoying! Caller ID helps screen calls to some degree.

Often, when the listed phone rings, I strongly suggest to Ed that he not answer so that I can determine whether a person who wants to speak to him has a real emergency. I don't always make a judgment, and not everyone will offer more than a name. Sometimes I sense that I should not ask any questions, and I simply call my husband to the phone. People who are quizzed sometimes become irate.

My point is that phone conversations can consume many hours of the day. I have worked so long on the boundary of not spending too much time on the phone that I have to nearly force myself to make necessary follow-up calls or to call people who are ill or friends with whom I need to keep in touch. Because there are many messages on the answering machine when I return home after several hours, I try to make the urgent return calls immediately; I am very thankful when people leave messages that do not require a response.

Filling the Calendar

There is a limit to how far ahead I will fill our social calendar. If someone wants to set a dinner date, I look at the family activities and check my husband's previously arranged schedule. His secretary and I are constantly in communication, talking through his schedule for several months at a time (not including specific appointments at the office). If I cannot see past an already packed season of school athletic events, I ask the person to call me in two months. I do not like to do this, and I try to let the person know that we would like very much to spend personal time with them; however, I cannot allow us as a family to have every day and night scheduled. The Christmas season, packed with parties and church activities, is especially busy.

I set a boundary regarding the attendance of weddings when we moved to Grand Rapids, and it has been met with some criticism. I felt that our children should not be expected to dress up for weddings unless they knew the couple and wanted to attend. When the children were young, I decided that if the children had one parent at a wedding nearly every week, they should not have both parents gone for every occasion; therefore I only would attend weddings of people I knew well. I recognized that as my children grew and I became personal friends with more people in the congregation, I could change that boundary.

My husband made a boundary for himself by not doing wedding rehearsals. He meets briefly with the couple in his office to talk over the specifics of the wording in the ceremony. The wedding committee handles all other aspects of the event. Otherwise, he would often have one more evening away from home.

Attendance at weddings, funerals, women's Saturday morning breakfasts (five or six a year), women's missionary meetings (once a month), women's special events (several times a year all day or in the evening), Tuesday women's Bible study, Wednesday evening choir rehearsals, Thursday prayer meetings, and extra choir rehearsals for special events, not to mention church on Sunday morning and evening, are just a few opportunities that come with some unwritten expectations and therefore are a challenge for boundaries. Although I am genuinely interested in what goes on in many areas, I am very open about not being able to attend every event. No lay church member expects herself or himself to attend every scheduled activity in the church, and realistically, neither should a layperson expect the pastor and/or his wife to do so. But once in a while I get a drift (as does my husband) that someone thinks one of us seems not to be interested in a certain area. Those people might understand our reasoning when they are gently reminded that, for example, if they do not work weekends, they can schedule things differently than our family.

Plans for schedule boundaries are not easily drawn when the church is small and the expectations are high. Ministry wives mentioned on the survey that one of the frustrations of their role was that of having to attend functions such as wedding and baby showers. This is not an easy tradition to change and should not be started; it could turn into a monster, as I observed recently. A women's ministry director of a young church told me that women's ministry had offered baby showers for each woman; this worked when the church was small. Giving showers seemed like such a nice idea. It provided fellowship, a way for women to get to know one another, until it became a burden. By the time attendance reached three hundred, eight women were pregnant at the same time. Questions rose as feelings surfaced: How can each person afford this? Should showers be given for women who keep having babies? What if the church keeps growing; do individuals dare not take part? While my advice was not sought, I gave it to the director anyway: Put a stop to this *now!* Help women who are genuinely in need, and let friends give friends showers. Let the church board handle this situation officially.

If you are unaccustomed to turning down any invitation, you may start by taking a gift to the hostess or guest of honor before the event, stating honestly that you need an evening at home. Honesty should be one of the basic values of your life anyway; do not make up a story about a situation that does not exist. In recent years I have heard myself using a new phrase: "I'm on overload!" Some people have actually thanked me for admitting that, because it has inspired them to say no when they feel their plate is too full.

Do Gifts Need Boundaries?

My mother warned me as a young pastor's wife not to become obligated to wealthy people who want to do things for us. Her framework of thinking was different from mine, and I do not wish to judge people's motives in giving; therefore, living out her directive is not easy, as she may have thought it would be. Some gifts are easily accepted, such as fruit baskets and magazine subscriptions; others give cause for soul-searching struggles. Sometimes we are reminded by givers that by our refusing the gift we deprive the giver of the joy of giving! This is a principle I often ponder, especially when I want to do something for someone who refuses to accept my offer.

What are we teaching our children when we accept gifts? We desire that they develop a sense of gratitude but do not want them to grow up expecting people to hand everything to them. As a pastor's child, my husband sensed that gifts given to him and his sister at Christmas were given because people felt sorry for their family having little money. I choose to believe that more often than not the giver simply wants to show appreciation to the Lord's servants for their dedication and service. Because we believe that we will be held accountable to God for the way we handle anything entrusted to us, we must seek God's face and respond in a way that will bring glory to him.

Family Privacy

Families handle their privacy boundaries in many ways. In Bernice Flynn's chapter of the book written by her husband, she states that he "prevented the invasion of our family privacy by never referring to us in sermons."[6] They had seven daughters, and that fact alone could have made for some interesting illustrations!

Ed asks permission before he tells a story related to one of our family members. The reverse from the Flynn's situation has occurred for us. Our two younger children have begged their father a few times to use a story they love: "Dad, when are you going to tell the 'broccoli story'?" They liked to hear the story more than the application of the illustration. As the children grow older, it is increasingly important not to embarrass them in front of their peers, especially if something that seems humorous to us is serious business to them. We have also discussed the prudence of not telling a story about a family member who may not be sitting in the service; later, as people pass the person in the church and make fleeting reference to the story, the person who is the subject of the story may be confused if he or she is unaware of what was told and could easily feel that his or her privacy has been invaded.

If your husband/pastor is not already sensitive to this issue, discuss it with him privately and suggest that he find out how the children feel. Remind him that this could save hurt feelings that could lead to unpleasant family relationships. After your private discussion, perhaps if you announce plans for an open family discussion to be held at a special meal or picnic, the children will enjoy feeling important for being able to share their feelings on this matter.

How Real Can I Be?

Sometimes people say sarcastically, "Lorna, I wish you could express to us a little more clearly what you think!" While I try to season these moments with a bit of the wisdom and humor I have gained over the years of letting my openness get me in trouble, they are avenues for allowing people to see that I am not hiding parts of my life. I have tried not to develop a separate private life from a public one, although as I mentioned earlier, I have not been entirely open about discussing my home-based business.

The flip side is that because I am the pastor's wife, I may not tell anyone in the congregation when I have a grievance about a staff issue or a matter of church policy or discipline. Ministry wives may feel strongly about church issues, but because we are not "regular" church members who have a right to voice an opinion (even if we can vote), we are limited in what we can say. I rarely have a problem living with that boundary, knowing that for those times when I wish to speak but cannot be heard, only my husband knows how I really feel. It is necessary for me to exercise discretion at all times. After all, if I am a true servant of the Lord, my opinion does not matter as much as my doing his will.

The American Dilemma

For several years I corresponded with a missionary whose children had no opportunities for church-structured programs with group activities or sports. She "talked through" the balance they had to find in developing their children's interests as well as taking part in ministry-related events. They were in a British-style education system, which puts much more pressure on students at age eleven than our children experience.

Conversely, when I wrote to her, I "talked through" the balance we tried to find in limiting the choices our children face, even on ministry teams. We put boundaries on our children's activities for their own health and for my driving time and sometimes for financial reasons. Parents usually know how much a child can take before physically breaking down, but do we practice the same restraint in our own lives, or are we driven by the desire and expectations of others to "be there" for everyone?

My missionary friend saw the upside of American activity; I saw the downside. She reminded me of the almost limitless resources we have for opportunities; I reminded her to treasure the quality and quantity time she has with her children. We both know that seeking God's wisdom in every situation is important and that no matter where we are on the globe, we must make responsible boundary decisions for the family.

Y'all Come

A few women indicated on the survey that their home has a "revolving door" or that the coffee pot is always on. One stated that their door had always been open, even before they entered ministry twenty-two years ago, and that it had rarely been abused. Only four said that their home is seldom open to others, either because of the wife's work or because the husband needs his home just to be home.

Nearly every other respondent fit somewhere between those two extremes when answering the question of her involvement in hospitality. Many ministry wives love to entertain and find creative ways to manage within their limitations of space, time, comfort zone, and physical challenges (some can't visit other people's homes because of allergies). Many pastors' homes are used for nearly every kind of small group ministry. Other ministry families, because of their children's ages, entertain mainly friends of the children. A few mentioned hosting neighbors and new families in the community.

Frequency of entertainment varies through the seasons of the year for us since we live on a private road with a curve and a hill that requires careful Michigan maneuvering in winter. We rarely invite crowds out to our home then. Even though people respect our privacy and rarely "drop in," I am usually delighted when someone feels comfortable enough to visit unexpectedly. At that time I try not to apologize for the condition of the home; it always looks lived in!

Schedule . . . Balance . . . Expectations

Nearly every area I have touched in this book can be viewed as an area to be given boundaries. Boundaries are not established just for privacy; they are to help you maintain balance in life. They can be adjusted through each season of life to help you make time for keeping yourself on an even keel so that you can be an effective disciple. All the parts of our lives develop into a tapestry but never without difficulty and never without the threads on the underside looking like a mess. The work must be done alone with the Lord as each of us accepts the responsibility for the choices we make in our lives. The boundaries we choose will help us achieve balance in our schedules and help us deal with the expectations placed on our lives. The boundaries we place around the importance of our time with the Lord will help us develop the relationship we long for with the One who loves us unconditionally and gave himself sacrificially.

Boundaries are simply limits to protect us from being overcome by things that are not in and of themselves evil but are "opportunities" that can drain our effectiveness. We will never be insulated from pain or protected from difficulty; that is not the goal for the Christian life and certainly not the goal for life in the ministry. No person is pain-free or trouble-free. If we were, we could not be effective ministers. Each of us is "called to be the wounded healer, the one who must look after his own wounds but at the same time be prepared to heal the wounds of others."[7]

In conclusion, I urge you to know your limits, strive to live within them, but never limit the power of the One who can meet your needs, take you beyond your limitations, and use you in spite of those limitations. If your boundaries are picket fences instead of concrete walls of separation, you will still be able to see and hear the needs of others and even keep the lines of communication open without feeling that you must meet their needs. Only God can do that.

Action Points

- Crying for some "personal space"? Take a quick survey of your personal and family boundaries. If the exercise is confusing or you make spiritual-sounding excuses for not having boundaries, set out on a mission to learn, to decide, and to act on what you learn about boundaries. Revisiting this periodically will help you move your boundaries as your life changes.

- Do you feel that you have this area of life in balance? Begin praying for pastors' wives who are distraught, over-burdened, and close to burnout trying to do everything their husbands and people in their churches expect of them.

Chapter 9

Husband Support
Being in His Corner

THIS CHAPTER WAS NOT PART OF THE FIRST EDITION
of this book. Having talked with ministry
caregivers about their frequent conversations
with pastors' wives and how they can be a support for their husbands, I prayed for an opportunity
to make this addition. In a conversation with Beverly
Hislop, who mentors wives of seminarians at Western
Seminary in Portland, Oregon, we discussed the fact that we
did not know of any current books covering this topic. I
asked her to pray about my including it in a future edition. As
I walked and prayed before finalizing the manuscript, I was
searching for words—what to call the chapter and how to
introduce it without sounding trite. I stopped at our mail-
box as I ended my walk, and in it was a beautifully
designed card published by a woman in our church
who is about my age and recently widowed. I
was so stunned at her insight into our situation that I called her immediately
and asked if I could use

several of her sentences to let you know how important I think this subject is:

> You are invaluable to him. Having you in his corner bolsters him physically, emotionally, and spiritually. You are his chief encourager, listener, and you both create, and are a "safe" place for him. It's a daunting role. It can be energy-draining and frustrating for a variety of reasons.
>
> So I pray for Ed, but also especially for you—for strength, energy, patience, and comfort. I pray that you will feel God's upholding presence standing beside you as you stand beside Ed.

The publishers put a great deal of thought into naming this book. Although I did not intend it to be solely about identity issues, they thought the title would catch the eyes of pastors' wives. I hoped the subtitle *Supporting Your Husband's Ministry Without Losing Your Identity* would speak to the need for a life fuller than one solely and completely wrapped up in the church. Although I had woven throughout the book thoughts on supporting husbands/pastors, I wanted to be more specific. I wrote a short list of ways I think I support Ed. Then I asked him to listen as I read the list and to tell me if what I do really is supportive and to add what he needs. Keep in mind that no matter what else I have written about support in this book, praying for our husbands should be top priority. And being their best friend and lover "for better, for worse" is also assumed. That established, here's my list:

- Encourage him regarding his preaching as well as ideas he develops for reaching people with the gospel.
- Try to make Sundays as easy as possible for him:
  1. by having meals prepared when he needs them or by eating out if that is more convenient.
  2. by reducing household noise and monitoring phone calls to protect his nap time.
- Don't resent Sundays not being "free" for doing things that some other families do.

- Convey to our children throughout life that when Dad has to be away from us for emergencies and regular meetings, this is part of God's call to ministry.
- Take care of our children (since I am writing this after they have passed childhood, the reader can assume I mean this in age appropriate ways).
- Do his laundry and have his clothes ready when he needs them (yes, I have forgotten at times).
- Listen.
- When possible, take part in ministry with him.

Ed's response warmed my heart! He said that all of these things on my list are secondary to my personal attitude. Because I felt called to ministry myself, I have been accepting of his call enthusiastically. This conversation took place after nearly thirty years of marriage. While we were dating, Ed shared with me his call to ministry, and since then we have developed the habit of discussing our hopes and dreams. H. B. London and Neil B. Wiseman expressed better than I can the importance of a couple's developing an agreed upon view of ministry:

> Whatever effort it takes for both of you to understand the meaning of ministry will be worth it. Together you must become aware of the key assumptions the pastor/spouse holds about ministry. To accomplish that, both of you must move beyond traditional views of ministry to determine what the work of God means to both of you. This may require looking past long-held notions about ministry and considering how the pastor/spouse personally views the essentials. In the process, the supporting husband or wife must guard themselves from saying, "Ministers don't talk or think that way." Let your partner talk, freely and creatively and even passionately, so you can understand and feel what his or her ministry is about.[1]

We can and must be supporters of our husband's call to ministry; otherwise we will not be completely one in the Lord. It will not happen alone by hoping, but by openly talking to one another, not just once, but as many times as is necessary throughout life, as both wife and husband grow spiritually and emotionally.

The following list of support ideas was compiled by pastors' wives in Sioux Falls, South Dakota. My comments are in italics.

1. Compliment something in the service within the first ninety minutes afterward: message, illustrations, or something else.

2. Look your husband in the eye as you listen to him. If he doesn't feel like talking, show your support by not trying to force him to talk. *(It may be appropriate to say that in some instances you do not know how to be supportive but that you care about what he thinks and feels and will be available when he is ready to talk.)*

3. Ask, "How can I help you?"

4. Say, "Remember I am praying for you."

5. Affirm him in his various roles: husband, father, grandfather, "fixer-upper."

6. Sit next to him in church. *(Obviously, this may not be appropriate at all times, especially if he is on the platform before he speaks. Know your church situation to determine this.)*

7. Write him an encouraging note (in his lunch, through the mail, email, answering machine, voice mail on his cell phone, etc.).

8. Verbalize, "I love you."

9. Help him light a fire under his dreams. Don't throw water on them.

10. Seek and do something fun with him—he needs a playmate. *(This point probably deserves a whole chapter about the need for clergy marriages to be healthy and whole! Kidnap him after you check his schedule to make sure he is free; take him to a new restaurant, bed and breakfast, or any kind of getaway. This should reduce stress, not cause it.)*

11. Say thank you to him, not only when you are alone, but in the presence of others.

12. Be on time for meals or for leaving the house. *(Some of you are laughing right now, because you are the only one who makes sure the dog is in, the lights are out, and the butter is covered so the cat won't lick it, etc.)*

13. Ask questions to help understand his needs: "Do I sound like your mother or your lover?"

14. Initiate loving touches.

15. Communicate that it is a privilege to serve with him.

16. Point out to the children his great qualities.

17. Appreciate his temperament (think on the positives of that temperament).

18. Notice the steps he takes to move forward.

19. Smile at him.

20. Do not complain through the difficulties.

21. Take his day off with him. *(Leave room for flexibility.)*

22. Compliment him on the things he does that nobody ever sees (checking the church buildings and sound system, opening windows, etc.).

23. Do not nag.

24. Be intimate; let the children see loving affirmations, touches.

25. Prepare a warm bubble bath for him. *(That wouldn't go over big at our house!)*

26. Be proud of him.

27. Give him space.

28. Honor his quiet—even if I am present. *(Just because he may be around the house does not mean he should be doing something. He needs time to think, rethink his sermons, process difficult appointments he has had, read, do nothing, "be still and know God.")*

29. Encourage him in his hobbies. *(If he has none, make an attempt to foster development of abilities or talents he may not use often; but do not nag.)*

30. Be patient.

31. Be forgiving.
32. Give unconditional support.
33. Send him flowers or a cookie bouquet.

In addition to these practical ideas, a pastor's wife can and should encourage her husband not to bear all of his burdens alone. He may be physically and emotionally drained by some parishioners who want his full attention after every service. If more than one person is demanding or critical, the pastor may become debilitated or depressed, feeling that no matter how hard he tries, he cannot meet these people's needs or demands. There are always people who need the pastor's attention, but if you see that someone or several people are constantly waiting to see your husband as soon as a service ends, encourage him to ask the church board for help. Elders or staff members could be available to help these people so that the pastor can turn his attention to someone who is seeking spiritual help because of the content of the sermon or is in crisis at that moment.

Ministers who are badgered or harassed by people who continually criticize his sermon content (when there is no doctrinal problem between the pastor and the board) should allow the board to confront these trouble-stirrers, especially if he has tried unsuccessfully to deal with the problem alone. Sometimes relentless arguers become stalkers and even put the pastor's family in danger. Such a situation should not be shouldered alone, and the pastor's wife can encourage her husband to solicit appropriate help. Otherwise, he may succumb to self-doubt and pity, thereby letting the enemy gain a foothold. This matter is magnified if a person tells the pastor that "God has told" him or her that the pastor should do something specific or threatens the pastor with the consequences of not following what he or she asserts.

Once when I was engaged in a radio interview, I was astounded by a caller's statement. He said that if pastors would just preach the Bible and stay true to the Word, people would not be critical. He felt that pastors get their feelings hurt all too often, and they just need to quit wanting so much attention. I was glad the host did not ask me to respond, although later in the program I was able to insert at an appropriate moment that "just preaching the Word" does not insure the absence of criticism! Obviously the caller had never been on the front line of spiritual warfare that a pastor experiences every Sunday. As Ed's wife, I need to encourage his commitment to staying true to the Word.

That Was a Nice Sermon, But . . .

Some wives of ministers can dish out criticism as well as their critics can. They have the "gift" of criticizing their husbands' sermons. How and when criticism is given will have a bearing on how it is received. Poor timing—for instance, bugging one's husband about a minor detail immediately following a service when he needs quiet, will only contribute to the wearing down of his spirit.

Having minored in English, I used to feel "called" to correct my husband with my grammatical expertise. Early in our marriage I thought I could "help" Ed by pointing out grammatical weaknesses in his sermons. He seldom acknowledged or applied my corrections. Eventually I gave up. His mistakes are few, and the fact that he can logically put together a sermon in a way that everyone can understand and remember—sometimes for years— tells me that pickiness is simply that. Besides, some of our church members have graduate degrees in the language, and if they choose to point out grammatical errors to him, either in jest or seriousness, he is more likely to take it from them than from me if I sound like a "constant dripping on a rainy day" (Prov. 27:15).

Women can encourage their husbands in a variety of ways, but we need to be cautious that our encouragement does not cause our husbands to feel pushed. I felt this caution in my spirit during September 2001. Ed had been planning for several months to preach through the book of Revelation on Sunday nights during September and October. Suddenly we were offered an incredible opportunity to visit sites in Turkey where the seven churches in Revelation are known to have been. It did not seem like good timing, but we thought perhaps we should make it work. Some people would be critical that he was leaving town just as the fall programs were getting started; but if they knew how it would enhance the sermon series, maybe they would understand. On the other hand, we did not have in mind care-givers for our son who was starting advanced subjects in high school. Would someone else make sure he was using his time wisely and completing and turning in his homework? We tried to weigh every possibility, think through every reason why we could or should go, and tried to minimize the negatives. Should we give up what looked like the opportunity of a lifetime? After all, it would help Ed's ministry!

One day during this internal wrestling, I called Ed and said that I did not want him to take my encouragement about the possibilities of going as an attempt to manipulate him if he felt we shouldn't go. After all, I wasn't feeling that we must make the trip and wouldn't be disappointed if we didn't. He said simply, "Thank you, that relieves me." Almost instantly he made the decision that it was not the right time to be gone. We were both relieved but didn't know why. We discussed our thoughts that even if we never knew on this side of heaven why we were saying no, we felt we were doing the right thing. We didn't want the people who offered the trip to think we were ungrateful, but we felt that if we missed the trip of a lifetime, that was all right. As it turned out, we would have been gone from September 8 through September 18, but we were home on September 11, 2001, the day that changed ministry in America.

Not only did we have more prayer meetings at church that week than usual, but people who had not thought previously about their own destinies came to the church seeking help. Ed and I both knew that it was right for us to have stayed home (although this story in no way faults people who were away from their homes or ministries at that time). One confirmation for me came from a conversation with a person in the community who does not attend our church. I had prayed for opportunities to share my faith with her and was able to begin that when she posed a question. She had seen a group of people on TV discussing whether, in light of the dangers of terrorism, one should have children, and also how parents should talk to their children regarding the attacks in New York City and at the Pentagon. She asked me whether I would parent differently if my children were young today. After my instant cry for wisdom from the Holy Spirit as I answered, I told her that when my children were young and expressed fear, we recited Psalm 56:3, "When I am afraid, I will trust in you." I said that I would teach our children now as then that God is trustworthy in good and bad times. Ed has often said that we should not blame God or judge him negatively based on one event. Letting children see our example of striving to trust God through life's most difficult times would say more than our words. I added that people have made and continue to make evil choices to harm other people, but God is still trustworthy. Our brief discussion opened a door for future talks. The Lord placed other people in my path with whom I could speak more freely about peace with God than before September 11.

Another way the pastor's wife can support her husband is through the relationship with his secretary (if the wife is not his secretary). Ed has always established early in the interview process that the relationship with his secretary will be business-like. Through our thirty years of marriage, he has had very few secretaries. Even though I love each of them dearly, it is clear that we maintain a relationship that will help Ed avoid opportunities for anyone to think that there are any openings for inappropriate emotions or actions between him and his secretary. He has also made it clear before hiring a secretary that, even though he is her pastor, if she needs long-term help with relationships at home, it is best to seek counseling through someone else. Having a trustworthy secretary is of utmost importance for many reasons: the privacy of the pastor's family, the confidentiality of people with whom the pastor counsels, and much more. If the pastor's wife is confident in knowing the character of her husband as well as his secretary (also called administrative assistant in some churches), life will go more smoothly in the parsonage.

Ed's secretary and I work together in one way that I feel is an important aspect of my supporting his ministry in touching people's lives. It began with my love for letter writing. I help provide a personal touch from the pastor's family that my husband does not have time to do. Our seventy-two missionaries receive tapes of our church services, and I have written all at least one letter telling them about the personal side of our family. Since I cannot possibly continue regular correspondence with all of them (and they are already on correspondence overload), I sometimes respond briefly to their email prayer letters. In recent years, I have had frequent or periodic contact with many whom I have come to know and love.

Realizing that I could devote too much time to missionaries all over the world and neglect the members here at home, I asked a staff wife to help me devise a way of touching people in our congregation. I was trying to do this by writing notes to people, but I kept falling behind. And the cost of wedding, get-well, sympathy, congratulations, and other special events cards as well as postage was becoming prohibitive. Church stationery didn't seem suitable, so my friend suggested that I request that the church purchase personalized stationery for Ed and me separately as well as together. I felt awkward and hesitated to do this, but with a little encouragement from my husband, I took the step. It was quickly approved! Now, years later, the stationery is printed on the church computers at very little cost. I have devised a system for personalizing notes for various occasions, and Ed's secretary keeps it on her computer. Now, for example, when birth announcements appear in the bulletin, she prints out a note of congratulations and Ed and I sign it. Sometimes I ask her to send persons with chronic illnesses a note so they will know we have not forgotten them even though we may not have seen them for a long time. This has helped ease the frustration of not being able to know everyone as I would like to. Attempting to reach out during moments of need or elation says that we care.

Some ministry wives spend a few hours each week in the ministry office doing this labor of love. If you are interested in such a ministry and need help with it, pray about it, let others know, and most likely someone will come forward with time and ideas to help you.

When Sin Ruins the Ministry Couple's Life

In spite of all the encouragement and support pastors' wives give their husbands, some ministers make sinful choices and default morally. This sobering thought brings to mind the scriptural caution, "So, if you think you are standing firm, be careful that you don't fall!" (1 Cor. 10:12). According to Linda Riley, the wife may, in her shock, "cover" for her husband, experience conflict of loyalties to God and to her husband, or she may be immobilized by feeling helpless, thinking no one will believe her, fearing the loss of their livelihood and home, or worse, being blamed as the cause or "whistleblower."[2] The wife may be able to play a part in the restoration of the marriage; however, she may need the help of a counselor in confronting and dealing with the situation. Tragically, some situations include verbal, emotional, and physical abuse, drug and substance abuse (even for prescription drugs), pornography, and other marriage problems. If the marriage is not reflecting the biblical principle of Christ loving the church (Eph. 5:25–30), earnest prayer is crucial for the one who needs to take action in the restoration process. See the appendix for resources.

"Don't Tell Your Wife"

Janice Hildreth, who writes an online newsletter for pastors' wives, has addressed another issue. When power struggles occur in the church, sometimes people try to make believe they have a special relationship with the pastor by manipulating confidentialities inappropriately with a statement like this: "Don't tell anyone, not even your wife (husband)," or "Let's just keep this between ourselves." Pastors' wives should be as trustworthy as their husbands when it comes to keeping confidences; however, the pastor and his wife would be well advised to take precautions for these potential setups. Hildreth says, "We [her pastor/husband and herself] see ourselves as one before God and therefore feel that free-flowing information is important to our ministry. That doesn't mean that we do share it, just that the confider needs to know there is a possibility we will share it with our spouse." Therefore, her husband usually asks the person why, letting the person know that he or she may be kept from gaining emotional superiority. "Manipulators exult in the feeling that comes from being privy to inside information that even the spouse doesn't know." However, the ministry couple praying together over the situation is better than the pastor alone praying. On the other hand, she says:

> This does not mean that there aren't situations, decisions and plans I don't know about. There are probably quite a few. Michael [her husband] is very wise in knowing what information I can emotionally handle and what needs to be kept to himself. So it's not that I have to or do know everything, it's that when a situation arises in which little antenna go up and common sense demands: why shouldn't my spouse know this? that we civilly inquire, why not? Just something to think about.[3]

"It's Not Your Fault"

Sometimes it is difficult for the pastor's wife to know how to encourage her husband when people leave the church, especially if the reasons for their leaving are not known. It is difficult enough when the reasons are known, especially when conflict is involved, but at least that information aids the pastor in bringing closure to the situation. Pastors are not superhuman, and there may be times when a pastor says or does something to offend and incite people to leave the church. But at other times the pastor's actions may have nothing to do with someone leaving the church. For instance, a couple stopped at our table to talk to us while we waited for our food at a restaurant. I had not seen them for a few months, but because our church has three morning services, I assumed they were there. The couple told us where they were presently attending church and why they had left our church. They held no ill feelings toward us or people in our church. It just "happened," and "God led them." We were cordial as they excused themselves when our food was served. Several issues passed through my mind as I processed what these people were saying and how it relates to my supporting my husband:

- This had nothing to do with Ed's preaching; they said they truly miss his sermons and the church. Even though we were aware of only a few facts, we did not need to take their change personally. Ed knows that he cannot meet everyone's needs and never will be able to do so. I encourage him to keep preaching the Bible, as he always has, in ways that are relevant, understandable, and applicable to listeners of all ages and backgrounds.

- The statement "God led us" cannot be refuted. Even if they had left because of a conflict with people, we wouldn't have had input into the resolution of the situation because we were uninformed. We feel that by someone's stating that God led them, the discussion comes to an end, since it would be inappropriate for us to say that God did not lead them to make the change.

- Culturally, we try to accept the fact that people change churches often. There are over five hundred Protestant churches in our area, and that provides a "cafeteria style" menu for some people. Personally, it is beyond my comprehension how some people pick, choose, and change churches. Many never settle and become fully involved because they are continually looking for the right place to meet their needs. Some people attend several churches at the same time, going to a variety of services and Bible studies, not just on Sundays, but throughout the week. There is no Bible verse to indicate that this is wrong, but it reflects an instability in our transient society and age.

- Even if we are slandered when people change churches, we should "answer kindly" (1 Cor. 4:13). This ministry isn't about us, about our wanting to feel good about ourselves; it is about "Christ crucified: a stumbling block to Jews and foolishness to Gentiles" (1 Cor. 1:23). My main encouragement to Ed is sometimes a reminder to both of us to refocus on what really matters.

- Let's be practical: Our church is not for everyone and not necessarily for all present attendees for their whole lives. Our parking lot has a limited number of spaces; people get fed up with traffic problems and shuttle service. In some churches problems may become magnified when everyone knows everyone else's business, whereas in a church like ours, getting lost in a crowd could be a positive or negative.

- People do experience hurt during conflict, whether intentionally or unintentionally. As servants of Christ, we can point them to him and his Word but cannot resolve every situation to everyone's satisfaction. This is the "hard stuff" in ministry life. While we love people deeply and invest our lives in them, we often must release to God our expectations for their lives. We must allow God to extend his grace through us and forgive offending parties. Sometimes as pastors' wives we want people to release their expectations of us; we owe the same to others. Of course there are times when conflict can lead to the parting of ways and result in positive changes.

As we discussed the conversation with that couple, I offered Ed a few encouraging words about his ministry, even though I did not think that he was feeling "down" because of it. I just wanted him to know I am in his corner. Several months later, the couple returned to our church.

Action Points

- Does your husband roll his eyes or bow his head while you tell people his faults? Do you call your put-downs "just being realistic"? Work on a specific way each week to let him know you appreciate the good things he does and the godly qualities he has. You may need to repent of being his opponent.

- If you think your husband feels that you are already supportive, ask him if there are any areas in which you may not have noticed his need for more support from you.

Chapter 10

Support Group
Custom Designing Your Own

IF YOU ARE FEELING PROMPTED TO BEGIN A SUPPORT group for pastors' wives, perhaps now is the time. Support groups start because of the vision of one person. If you are already part of a group but feel the need to refresh or revive one that is beginning to die, you may be ready to take a step of faith and leadership that will be a source of encouragement to other pastors' wives. If, however, you feel no need or desire to be part of a support group at this time, read on anyway. I have not been part of a support group for several years, and I do not believe that anyone should be pressured to be part of one. There are already enough pressures in ministry life!

Numerous Bible passages support the idea of encouraging, helping, edifying, and comforting one another (for example, 2 Cor. 1:3–4), but the purpose of this chapter is not to teach a Bible lesson. We have already noted that Jesus had a small group of friends, as well as a peer group, called disciples, whom he taught and trained in spite of the fact that they were not perfect. Sometimes we as Christians are afraid to develop relationships with people outside our "group." We pastors' wives may be afraid to be in a support group if there are women from churches different from ours. We may be afraid of our own ignorance regarding the beliefs and practices of others, or we may be afraid that our belief system might be tainted by our acquaintance with someone who interprets the Bible differently.

When you start or become part of a support group, you should know whether the group is open to all denominations, religions, or cults. This could become an evangelistic outreach avenue for you if you are open to having women attend who need fellowship but may not yet know Christ as Savior. If you initiate the group, you can let women "know that Christ is the center and the Bible is your guide."[1]

My husband has often mentioned that when a group of pastors get together there is a tendency to say, "How many are you running?" My friend Linda Riley says that sounds like herding cattle, not shepherding sheep! Pastors' wives' support groups should not be about comparing numbers, budgets, buildings, or anything else related to ecclesiastical status. However, because some of these issues factor into our needs or problems shared within the group, only those facts necessary to explain a specific situation should be discussed as the friendships and trust are built. Women from every size and type of church need support, because the church is full of needy people.

Benefits of a Support Group

1. Deep fellowship (a result of biblical love)—developed as you build trust and openness. This group will discuss the realities of ministry.
2. Close friendship with a few. A support group is much more than a pity party.
3. A sense of "belonging"—the opposite of the loneliness you may be experiencing in your church. Making re-

sources available (listed in appendix) will help lonely women realize many pastors' wives are dealing with similar issues.

4. A place for objectivity. In this group you may share your current dilemma and group members can see the larger picture, giving you perspective when you have been blind-sided by a situation. Sometimes you need to be pointed to Jesus.

5. A place for concrete thinking and problem-solving. Women with experience are very happy to share ideas and resources as well as warn you if your intended solution may lead to disaster.

6. Camaraderie among ministry couples that may ward off some gossip among church-hoppers.

7. An alternative to expensive group therapy. Sisters can help you sort through healthy ways to deal with conflict. This may involve your church situations, but as true friendships develop, you will also discuss other facets of life.

8. The comforting feeling of being uplifted in prayer. Praying for one another will come naturally as you establish friendships.

A word of caution: A pastor's wife might learn biblical truth from another's ministry by being in a support group. Differences of biblical interpretation can cause marital problems for a ministry couple, which is not the goal or a benefit of a support group, and these situations must be handled prayerfully.

One of my friends whose parents were in ministry for many years reminded me that the older generation would not discuss ministry problems. She said, "Maybe the reason our parents' generation doesn't talk is because they had no training or support and withdrew. They were expected to be mature without the years of experience." If you are part of a support group, you may actually experience training or mentoring by the group. This could be a gift from the Lord, whether or not you have experienced formal training. If you are one of the older women in the group, this is your opportunity to invest in younger women, especially if you have a positive attitude about it. Rather than thinking that you are too old to relate to the younger generation, remember that your godly wisdom can be a source of inspiration and hope.

Examples of Types of Groups

If you are forming a new group, discuss with a few pastors' wives you know or invite to your first informational meeting what kind of group they would like to become. If you are willing to be flexible, you may experiment until you find the right style of fellowship you want to form. Knowing your community culture will help you decide.

1. Book discussion. Choose a book about Christian living or ministry life and discuss the chapters or issues in the book. Possibly invite the author (if local) or a guest speaker who is available and knowledgeable about that topic.
2. Luncheon/dinner. Brown-bagging lunch and exchanging prayer requests on cards may be necessary for women who work, or an open-ended evening at a restaurant may work.
3. Only for fun. One pastor's wife told me that her group meets to shop; golf; do a craft or clothes exchange; give each other manicures, pedicures, and facials; or stay overnight at a camp. They enjoy variety.
4. Once-a-year dinner with spouses or family picnic.

Where Do I Start?

- Pray.
- Listen to God through his Word, through circumstances, and through the prompting of the Holy Spirit.
- Talk to your husband. Agreement with him about this venture will be a blessing.

- Enlist one or two pastors' wives to help you start. Call a church, introduce yourself, and ask for the pastor's wife's name and number if you do not know another pastor's wife.
- Find out through other churches if pastors' wives know of support groups already established.
- Meet with a few women to discuss issues, such as:
  1. Location. Find a place where there is privacy, where confidential matters can be discussed freely.
  2. Whether you need a facilitator/moderator. After the group is established, each person should take part in hostessing or contributing in some way, whether in giving a devotional, leading prayer time, or something else. One woman should not have the final word on or responsibility for everything.
  3. Whether any ministry wife will be invited, or only senior or solo pastors' wives.
  4. Size of the group. About twelve is maximum for developing serious relationships.
  5. Time limit and frequency of meetings (for example, once a month or every other month). The facilitator would need to help the group keep to the time limit, probably an hour to an hour and a half.
  6. Who will call or send invitations (anything that involves cost should be shared by the whole group).
  7. Who will provide drinks and/or snacks (rotation is good for any job mentioned).
  8. Expectations. Women who decide to attend should make a commitment for a year or a school year, making the group a priority so that true fellowship and relationships can be developed. As I said at the beginning of the chapter, anyone who is not so inclined should not be considered part of the group. Confidentiality should be a key component. An occasional attendee can disrupt the confidence built in deep conversations among women who attend regularly. Each

person is expected to participate, with courtesy of listening being as important as sharing. This includes emotional involvement, something that cannot be attained by one who attends occasionally.

Suggestions for Prayer Time

It hardly seems necessary to write in a book for pastors' wives suggestions for handling prayer time in a fellowship group! However, any of us may get in a rut and therefore may benefit from changing our routine from time to time.

- Open the meeting with prayer or ask someone ahead of time to do it.
- Give everyone opportunity to share prayer requests. Prayer requests are limited to immediate family or personal concerns since time constraints prohibit requests for everyone known to everyone in the group.
- Begin the prayer time with sentence prayers of praise and adoration.
- Two or three turn toward one another to pray in small groups at times and at other times remain in a large circle.
- Each person brings her own prayer journal or paper to write requests and remembers to pray regularly for group members.
- Feel free to stop the conversation at any time during the meeting and pray for a specific concern being discussed by a group member. With her permission, encircle the person and touch her shoulder or take her hand as the group prays.
- Give the option to kneel or sit during prayer time.
- Allow for freedom if a person wishes to sing a song in worship during prayer time; however, sensitivity is needed if women in the group are unfamiliar with the song.

Don't Just Sit There, Get Together

All of these suggestions are simply that. Help your group take on its own personality and style, guiding it to be a meaningful time together, not simply a social gathering for discussing the latest TV programs. I have friends with whom I share moments of laughter and moments of crying over life's deep difficulties. After I've been with them, I feel that it has been time well spent, valuable and uplifting. That is what a support group should impart. If a woman gives up time with her family, she should feel when she returns home that it was worth her time and effort, because being part of the support group helps her become a better person. Not only should she benefit, but her husband and family should benefit from the ripple effect.

Action Points

- Decide whether you need support or want to be isolated. Like boundaries, leave this area open for change, especially if you sense that you could offer support to others even though you may not feel the need for group dynamics.

- Take time at least once to get together with pastors' wives outside your region or denomination just to expand your appreciation for the dedicated lives of servants you would otherwise not meet.

Chapter 11

God's Glory
A Sure Calling

"SO, LORNA, HOW HAS YOUR YEAR BEEN?" THE
question was directed to me by a discon-
tented staff wife sitting at the far end of a
crowded table. She had made it clear to many
that she expected her husband to make more
money and that she wanted to live in the same style as
other family members who were in lucrative professional work.

"I don't know what kind of answer you're looking for,"
I responded. "Some days are wonderful and others are
lousy. But I am content that we are where God wants us to
be, and I am happy to be here. I have no dreams for any
other way of life."

There was a time when I pictured myself unmarried,
a music teacher in Hawaii, telling boys and girls
about the Lord. But even though I was willing
to go back there after a missions trip
in high school, I never felt a call to
do so, never experienced

any doors opening, and never had the urge to push the doors open. I did, however, hear a specific call through an invitation by Dr. John R. Rice in college chapel to surrender my will to be a pastor's wife, the one area of my life I had withheld. Knowing that God does not make mistakes when he calls helps me weather the storms of ministry life. Not only does he not make mistakes; he also faithfully fulfills his promises to those he calls (Num. 23:19; 1 Thess. 5:24).

I had a willing heart to serve God as a young person, but I had many rough edges that have taken years of daily trials and periodic storms to shape. The reason why I wanted to marry an evangelist and not a pastor was so that I would not have to stay anywhere long enough for people to know the real me with my imperfections. Maybe I wanted to appear to be perfect, but more likely, I knew that working on those imperfections would be uncomfortable. When I surrendered that area of my life, I knew that God could and would work through me no matter where I lived or what I did. (My husband and I were not yet dating at the time of that decision.)

Feel Like a Square Peg in a Round Hole?

It is common for people in ministry to make statements regarding what they could or could not do in certain settings. And it is not always because we know ourselves well or know where we "fit." Two contrasting statements I have heard are: "I couldn't handle being in a large church where you can't know everybody; I prefer a smaller group," and "I'm glad to be out of a small church where you see the same people every week and everyone knows everything about you!" These comments were obviously made by ministry people with different comfort zones. While they express honest thoughts, people who say such things may be unintentionally dismissing the power of God to assist them in finding their niche wherever he places them. Do we make our own comfort the goal of ministry? I have heard that Christians in countries where suffering for claiming the name of Christ is the norm pray for us easy-living Americans that we would know what it means to suffer for Christ's sake. If their prayers are answered, our lives in ministry definitely will not become any easier! I have wondered what those people thought or felt when terrorists attacked America on September 11, 2001. Ministry life changed that day in many ways. But that is a separate issue, and my aim is to leave you with words of encouragement to forge ahead wherever you are. Fulfillment in knowing you are doing what God called you to do is far better than merely feeling comfortable. Remember that ministry wives have as many different ways of ministering as there are personalities; no two "do ministry" exactly alike any more than their husbands.

Find Your Own Way to Minister

Although I have mentioned a number of specific ways pastors' wives can support their husbands, some readers may still be wondering where and how they can fit in. After all, ministry can seem overwhelming at times. If you find that you are having a struggle with fitting in, pray for ways to support your husband in ministry so that you will feel more a part of his life. As I shared in chapter 9, I support my husband and minister with him in various ways. I have never felt that his ministry should be totally separate from my life or ambitions. There was a time in ministry when I felt that my training in music was practically a dead issue in service, since I was not using or developing it, but I was completely convinced and content that we were where we belonged, where Ed felt God led us for that time. Later, when we moved, the music area of my life was resurrected. How I support and minister with Ed every day keeps changing with my own growth, with the changing times of our children, with experimentation in avenues of ministry as opportunities arise, and with the development of our marital relationship.

If God has led your husband into the ministry and you are one with him in the Lord, God's plan is for you to experience joy and fulfillment as well. Finding exactly how that works may require times of assessment, discussions with your husband, and possibly a willingness to become educated in fields unknown to you before entering ministry. It may also require years of searching the Word, journaling, and being still before the Lord as he develops your desires to fit into his plan. Stretching my memory, it seems that when I was young, a person went to college to get a degree to spend a lifetime using what was learned in college. Now it is common for a person to enter a vocation that is totally unrelated to his or her undergraduate degree. In a sense, that happened to me. I was a music education major with an English minor. For years I taught piano and was a church musician, having developed the talent as much as I could within the time frame I was willing to give to it. Now I have been almost completely out of the music ministry for more than three years, and I seldom play the piano at home, except to teach a song to my granddaughter. At this moment I am doing what I love to do—writing. Of course, I have personal contact with people through Bible study, work outside the home, networking, and church work. And with the approaching empty nest, I am able to spend more time with my husband as he ministers to people.

My point is that while we want to be "doing" what we love most, there are seasons of life when we are at rest just learning to "be" before our Father. It is important to realize that we change with the seasons, and in this journey we will be better women if we are not demanding to always be doing what we want, or what we think we want, to do. While we have defining moments in our lives, much of our spiritual development requires years of metamorphosing. Sometimes we just need to "chill" as we wait on the Lord to fulfill his plans through us.

What We Do . . . Who We Are

Throughout this book I have given examples of what we *do* in ministry. Who we *are* as "normal" human beings in a vocation that pays its employees (but not the wives of male employees) to *do* ministry is another facet of our lives for which we are accountable. If I act out my Christianity a certain way only because my husband is paid to be a full-time Christian worker, my values are mixed up. Many people in our church are employed by secular companies, yet they appear to me to be in full-time ministry. I say this for several reasons: They share the gospel with nearly everyone they meet. Everyone who comes to their home is ministered to by their lives. Almost every hour spent away from their vocation is dedicated to the building up of new Christians. And when they take a vacation, it is because they need a break from ministry as much as from their secular work, where they often minister as well. That is the kind of Christian and disciple I want to be—the kind who lives out my faith because I am full and overflowing with the Spirit of Christ. Having a Bible-centered background does not give me an "edge" on newer Christians in ministry. If I fail to avail myself of the power of Christ, making excuses for not witnessing because of apathy, rationalization, or fear, I will be held accountable.

Even ministry wives who did not expect or want to live in the "fishbowl" of pastoral ministry can follow the same principles. If you have settled the issue of accepting where God has placed you in life, you can "walk a step at a time in obedience to God's call [and] find that the power is there for that one step."[1] Further, you "ought to thank the Lord we don't know what's around the corner of tomorrow."[2] In the years ahead, ministry may grow even more complex than it is today. We can be thankful that God does not show us ahead of time.

Someone God Loves Is HIV Positive

One of the complexities that we have dealt with in ministry is HIV/AIDS. Scripture tells us that God is no respecter of persons, but sometimes we ministry people don't follow Christ's example in that area. Both the Old Testament prophets and Jesus himself ministered to the needs of those who had leprosy—the outcasts of their culture. Today's "outcasts" are those who have AIDS, and as Christ's ambassadors, we are called to minister to them. Churches must formulate a plan for ministering to the special needs of AIDS patients and their families.[3]

We know several ministry couples whose children have died of AIDS, one having contracted it through tainted blood transfusions and another through homosexual behavior. Because many people who converted from promiscuous lives have entered ministry, it is not outside the realm of reality that AIDS is entering the pulpit as well as the parsonage. Shall we be quick to turn our backs on our fellow ministers as well as our flock? Often we hear from someone who is touched by this dreaded killer. More often than not, most patients' family members defect emotionally and physically when they learn of the diagnosis, even if the patient is a professing Christian. Even more often, it seems, a family who professes Christianity will not tolerate communication with one who contracts AIDS because of a sinful lifestyle. What will we do with Mark 9:41, where Jesus says, "Anyone who gives you a cup of water in my name because you belong to Christ will certainly not lose his reward"? Will we not reach out to meet basic needs of the dying, whether they are born again or not? Should they not have the chance to make peace with God just like any other person? How will they hear if someone will not tell them (Rom. 10:12–15)?

When the Grand Rapids AIDS Resource Center had an open house, my husband and I attended the reception. One of our church members was on the board, and many HIV-positive and AIDS patients attended our Saturday night service, so it was natural for my husband to want to attend the opening. But this was a new, uncomfortable experience for me. I spent some time reading the brochures that were displayed and realized that I live in a shielded environment even though my husband has been reaching out to these hurting people for years. I was not prepared for ministry to a new (to me) world of suffering people, but I asked the Lord to break and mold my heart for possible future ministry.

Because I know that God has made no mistakes in the past, I am confident that he will make no mistakes in leading me in the days to come. I am concerned, however, when I hear that there are people in ministry denying the reality of the need for showing compassion to AIDS patients and their families. A friend told me that she organized a meeting for a group of ministry women; they had been invited to listen to the heartrending story of a person whose relative had recently died of AIDS. When everyone left immediately afterward without talking to the speaker, it seemed obvious that they felt the meeting was irrelevant to them. One pastor's wife said angrily to the organizer, "I don't know why you had this kind of meeting. None of us is going to have to go through this."

My desire is to warn you not to make the mistake of locking the door for ministry because of pride, anger, or hatred for or fear of those whom God brings to knock on it. If we do, we run the risk of finding that the doors we want him to open are locked and bolted.

Abuse in the Church

Another result of sin that complicates people's lives is abuse: physical, emotional, and spiritual abuse. This has become more evident as shelters have opened for abused adults and their children. Not all church leaders are prepared to deal with these issues, since legal matters, spiritual matters, and physical needs are combined into a huge crisis for many people. As I have learned about how devastating this is to families, I realize that I am unequipped to help, but I do have a responsibility to be able to refer a person in crisis to someone who can help. Sadly, many people in the church endure decades of abuse in their homes because of the perpetrators' misuse of Scripture. Pastors (and their spouses) who have not been trained to give support to victims often deny that the problem exists in their church, just as has been the case with AIDS. Some pastors fear that finding out who in their congregation is being abused will open doors to problems they do not know how to address. For pastors who do attempt, without proper training, to deal with couples involved in domestic violence, the problems are exacerbated, especially if pastors blame women for exaggerating their situation.[4]

The above mentioned issues are just a few of the societal problems that exist within our churches. As pastors' wives, we must not let ourselves go through life with blinders, uninformed or judgmental of people whose lives don't fit into our preconceived ideas of ministry life. We need to make work of educating ourselves. We may not be called to learn all the facets of helping everyone's needs (remember our boundaries?), but we do have an obligation to pray for and be willing to be used to help them if God leads them into our path.

"We Are Not Yet What We Shall Be"

Reflect for a moment on the apostle Paul's words: "And we, who with unveiled faces all reflect the Lord's glory, are being transformed into his likeness with ever-increasing glory, which comes from the Lord, who is the Spirit" (2 Cor. 3:18). What joy that emotes, when we look back a verse and see that "where the Spirit of the Lord is, there is freedom." The Spirit is with me now; I have freedom in him. My being a pastor's wife is merely a way for him to work through me as I reflect his glory! God doesn't make mistakes.

Someone gave my husband a beautifully framed statement by Martin Luther. Its message is that life is a journey and that Christianity is not a quick fix to perfection. We walk along a path from which the end cannot be seen. But we are never without hope of what exhilarating joy the destination will bring.

> *This life therefore is not righteousness*
> *but growth in righteousness*
> *not health but healing*
> *not being but becoming*
> *not rest but exercise.*

We are not yet what we shall be
  but we are growing toward it,
  the process is not yet finished
  but it is going on,
  this is not the end
  but it is the road.

All does not yet gleam in glory
  but all is being purified.

Action Points

Unless your family demands require your total involvement with them,

- Observe a new ministry, even if only to learn about a vision God has given to other servants.

- Take a risk in being part of a ministry you have thought about. Test the waters by working for three months in a new ministry or go on a short-term missions trip.

- Feel new life in your bones by letting go of something to which you may have been clinging too long. Revive your walk with the Lord while you wait for a new door of opportunity to open. "Be still, and know that [God is] God" (Ps. 46:10).

Resources

ONE OF MY MAIN CONCERNS FOR MINISTRY WOMEN HAS BEEN THE accessibility of information for resources. Half the women I surveyed during the early 1990s said they had no knowledge of caregivers whose sole ministry is to ministers and their spouses. They were also unaware that more general ministries often have branches that focus on the needs of ministry people. Below is a list of a few of these ministries and resources for finding more. I knew of no websites when the first edition of this book was printed; now many of them carry links to other ministries. Bear in mind that websites are changed often and may no longer be available by the time you read this.

Some ministries exist to help clergy couples but do not desire national exposure because of their limited space and personnel. If you obtain a directory of resources and begin contacting individuals, you may easily find help much closer to home than you anticipated. Caregivers network among themselves and are very helpful with referrals. Sometimes all you need is a little time and persistence as you open and read websites and links within them. Contact the person whose email is listed. If you do not own a computer, find a friend who is willing to help you access websites. Don't give up if you need help!

General Resources

Focus on the Family has a division called Pastoral Ministries, which produces "Pastor to Pastor," an audiotape series with a newsletter, available by subscription. Focus on the Family also publishes a Pastoral Care Directory for pastors and their families that includes books, videos, audiotapes, booklets, periodicals, leadership/conflict/financial/legal consultants, retreat centers, and counseling and treatment centers. When calling the Pastoral Ministries Department, ask for Dr. H. B. London Jr. or Rev. Roger Charman.

Web: www.parsonage.org
London, H. B., Jr. *Pastors at Risk*. Wheaton, IL: Victor, 1993.
London, H. B., Jr., and Neil Wiseman. *Married to a Pastor: How to Stay Happily Married in the Ministry*. Ventura, CA: Regal, 1999.

Focus on the Family
P.O. Box 35500
Colorado Springs, CO 80935-3550
(719) 531-3360/1-800-232-6459 (A-FAMILY)
Pastoral Care Line: 1-877-233-4455

Partners in Prayer website is a ministry of Dr. John C. Maxwell and The INJOY Group to help pastors develop prayer partner ministries within their own churches. Also on this website is a Directory of Caregivers. Over twenty categories of caregiving ministries are listed, both by categories and by geographic location. A Directory Application is included for any ministry not already listed.

Web: www.pastorsnet.org

Just Between Us: The Magazine for Ministry Wives

Published quarterly by Telling the Truth Media Ministries. For subscription information, write or call:

Elmbrook Church
777 South Baker Road
Brookfield, WI 53045
1-800-260-3342

Web: www.justbetweenus.org
Email: jbu@elmbrook.org

The Pastor's Wife

An internet monthly interdenominational newsletter for women married to ministers.
8731 Brynwood Drive
Boise, ID 83704
Email: janicetpw@quest.net
Web: www.pastorswife.com

"Pastors' Wives" Support Board

Rock Dove Publications
Web: www.rockdove.com.pwsupport.html

Support and encouragement through prayer requests, devotionals, links to many other websites, and lists of current and out-of-print books by and for pastors' wives.

Web: www.geocities.com/Heartland/Pointe5892
Web: www.geocities.com/mamag7_2000

Ministry Wives Network, International (MINWIN)

MINWIN is a network of Christ-centered groups of pastors' wives who support one another as they face challenges of life in ministry. It exists to edify, encourage, equip, and educate ministry wives through national conferences and resources.

Contact: Lynne Dugan
37784 Pineknoll Avenue
Palm Desert, CA 92211
1-888-249-5782
Email: MINWIN4G@aol.com

Caring for People God's Way

A certificate program in biblical counseling, from the Center for Biblical Counseling, an external studies division of American Association of Christian Counselors.

1-800-520-2268
Web: www.aacc.net

For Further Reading

Heim, Pamela Hoover. *The Pastor's Wife: Balancing Her Multiple Relationships*. Eugene, OR: Harvest Publications, 2001.

A compilation of newsletter articles that may be used for personal meditation or group discussion.

Rubietta, Jane. *How to Keep the Pastor You Love*. Downers Grove, IL: InterVarsity Press, 2002.

For laypeople and clergy alike.

Toney, Luana R. *Paper Dolls Do Tear ... But God Is the Tape: A Devotional Guide of Restoration for Pastors' and Ministers' Wives.* Cedar Rapids, IA: Paper Doll Ministries, 2002.

Address: 1400 Parkwood Drive, S.E., Cedar Rapids, IA 52403.

Because developing our walk with the Lord is more important than any other relationship, I want to suggest a few books that have recently enhanced my journey:

DeMoss, Nancy Leigh. *A Place of Quiet Rest: Finding Intimacy with God Through a Daily Devotional Life.* Chicago: Moody Press, 2000.

Hazard, David. *You Set My Spirit Free: A 40-Day Journey in the Company of John of the Cross.* Minneapolis: Bethany House, 1994.

Korch, Steve. *My Soul Thirsts: An Invitation to Intimacy with God.* Valley Forge, PA: Judson Press, 2000.

Rubietta, Jane. *Quiet Places: A Woman's Guide to Personal Retreat.* Minneapolis: Bethany House, 1997.

____. *Still Waters: Finding the Place Where God Restores Your Soul.* Minneapolis: Bethany House, 1999.

Notes

Chapter 1

1. Roy M. Oswald, *Clergy Stress and Burnout Workbook* (Bethesda, MD: Alban Institute, Ministers' Life Resources, 1983), 23.
2. Anna E. S. Droke, *The Diary of a Minister's Wife* (New York: Eaton & Mains, 1914), 61–62.
3. Frances Nordland, *The Unprivate Life of a Pastor's Wife* (Chicago: Moody Press, 1972), 12.
4. Ibid., 13.
5. William Barclay, *The Letters to Timothy, Titus, and Philemon*, rev. ed. (Philadelphia: Westminster Press, 1975), 99.
6. Nordland, *Unprivate Life*, 14.
7. Homer A. Kent Jr., *The Pastoral Epistles* (Chicago: Moody Press, 1958), 132.
8. William Hendriksen, *New Testament Commentary: Thessalonians, Timothy and Titus* (Grand Rapids: Baker, 1957), 133.
9. Ruthe White, *What Every Pastor's Wife Should Know* (Wheaton, IL: Tyndale, 1986), 146.
10. Ibid.
11. Linda Riley, "Job Description for a Pastor's Wife: How to Write Your Own," published by Called Together Ministries, Torrance, California, 1997.

12. See Oswald Chambers, *My Utmost for His Highest: An Updated Edition in Today's Language* (Grand Rapids: Discovery House, 1992), December 12, on personality as the "characteristic mark of the inner, spiritual man."

Chapter 2

1. Jill Briscoe, *Renewal on the Run* (Wheaton, IL: Harold Shaw, 1992), 16–17.
2. Ibid.
3. Richard J. Neuhaus, *Freedom for Ministry,* rev. ed. (Grand Rapids: Eerdmans, 1992), 43.
4. Ibid.
5. Numerous books are available to help with the grind of everyday life. See the appendix at the back of this book for resources. See also Emilie Barnes, *The 15-Minute Organizer* (Eugene, OR: Harvest House, 1991), for suggestions for completing one task at a time.
6. See Pat and Jill Williams, *Rekindled* (Old Tappan, NJ: Revell, 1985), 70–76.
7. Briscoe, *Renewal on the Run,* 6–11.

Chapter 3

1. For further reading, see Edwin Friedman, *Generation to Generation* (New York: Guilford Press, 1985).
2. Bill and Lynne Hybels, *Fit to Be Tied* (Grand Rapids: Zondervan, 1991), 96.
3. Ibid., 98–99.
4. For further reading, see Dennis and Matthew Linn and Sheila Fabricant, *Healing the Eight Stages of Life* (New York/Mahwah, NJ: Paulist Press, 1988).
5. Lois Mowday, *Daughters Without Dads* (Nashville: Oliver Nelson, 1990), 73.
6. For further reading, see Donald E. Sloat, *Growing Up Holy and Wholly: Understanding and Hope for Adult Children of Evangelicals* (Brentwood, TN: Wolgemuth & Hyatt, 1990).
7. If you wish to work through a Bible study that addresses issues of the past, I recommend Beth Moore's *Breaking Free: Making Liberty in Christ a Reality in Life* (Nashville: LifeWay Press, 1999.)

Chapter 4

1. Oswald Chambers, *My Utmost for His Highest; An Updated Edition in Today's Language* (Grand Rapids: Discovery House, 1992), November 30.
2. For further reading, Bill and Lynne Hybels, *Fit to Be Tied* (Grand Rapids: Zondervan, 1991), chap. 9, "Whatever Happened to Romance?"
3. Edward B. Bratcher, *The Walk-on-Water Syndrome* (Waco, TX: Word, 1984), 95.
4. Stefan Ulstein, *Pastors [Off the Record]* (Downers Grove, IL: InterVarsity Press, 1993), 17–18.
5. Lorna Dobson, *Caring for Your Pastor: Helping God's Servant to Minister with Joy* (Grand Rapids: Kregel, 2001). I wrote on this and other related topics for laypeople in order to take some of the mystery out of what the pastor's life is really like, as well as to point out ways in which laypeople can minister to their ministers.

Chapter 5

1. Oswald Chambers, *My Utmost for His Highest; An Updated Edition in Today's Language* (Grand Rapids: Discovery House, 1992), November 5.
2. Carol Kent, *Secret Longings of the Heart* (Colorado Springs: NavPress, 1990), 117–121.
3. Bill and Lynne Hybels, *Fit to Be Tied* (Grand Rapids: Zondervan, 1991), 186–187.
4. Marjory F. Foyle, *Honourably Wounded: Stress Among Christian Workers,* rev. ed. (Mill Hill, London/Grand Rapids: Monarch Books, 2001), 13.
5. Diane Langberg, *Counsel for Pastors' Wives* (Grand Rapids: Zondervan, 1992), 199.
6. Ibid., 68.
7. The Navigators is an international Christian organization that produces tools for believers to learn biblical discipleship and then apply what they learn to their lives and ministries. (See the appendix for information.)
8. Ruth Myers, *31 Days of Praise: Enjoying God Anew* (Sisters, OR: Multnomah, 1994).

9. For further reading, Langberg, *Counsel,* chap. 14, "Where Can I Go for Help?"

10. Henri J. M. Nouwen, *The Wounded Healer* (New York: Doubleday, 1972), 84.

Chapter 6

1. Henry Cloud and John Townsend, *Boundaries: When to Say Yes, When to Say No to Take Control of Your Life* (Grand Rapids: Zondervan, 1992), 58.

2. Alfred L. Heller, *Your Body, His Temple* (Nashville: Thomas Nelson, 1981).

3. Renee Coates Scheidt, "Let's Get Physical," *Just Between Us,* Winter 2000, special section on "Taking Care of Yourself," 14.

4. Lorna Dobson, *Caring for Your Pastor: Helping God's Servant to Minister with Joy* (Grand Rapids: Kregel, 2001), 7.

5. Nancy Pannell, *Being a Minister's Wife and Being Yourself* (Nashville: Broadman, 1993), 145.

6. Ibid., 143.

Chapter 7

1. Ruth Tucker, *Multiple Choices* (Grand Rapids: Zondervan, 1992), 75–77, explains the difference between headship and submission.

2. Concepts are condensed from a sermon at Calvary Church, June 21, 1992, "Are Headship and Submission Relevant Concepts?"

3. Barbara Kay Mouser, *Five Aspects of Woman: A Biblical Theology of Femininity* (1997), a study course offered and published by the International Council for Gender Studies, P.O. Box 702, Waxahachie, TX 75168.

4. For indepth reading, see James R. Beck and Craig L. Blomberg, eds., *Two Views on Women in Ministry* (Grand Rapids: Zondervan, 2001).

5. Tucker, *Choices,* 77.

6. For further reading on knowing your own needs, which could lead to knowing and meeting each other's needs as a couple, see Bobb Biehl, *Why You Do What You Do* (Nashville: Thomas Nelson, 1993).

7. *Merriam-Webster's Collegiate Dictionary,* 10th ed. (Springfield, MA: Merriam-Webster, 1993), loc. cit.
8. Leslie B. Flynn, *How to Survive in the Ministry* (Grand Rapids: Kregel, 1992), 109.
9. Ibid., 110.
10. Linda Riley, "Serving Together," published by Called Together Ministries, Torrance, California, August 1993.
11. From a "Pastor to Pastor" tape from Focus on the Family.

Chapter 8

1. Henry Cloud and John Townsend, *Boundaries: When to Say Yes, When to Say No to Take Control of Your Life* (Grand Rapids: Zondervan, 1992), 149.
2. Ibid., 93–94.
3. Bill and Lynne Hybels, *Fit to Be Tied* (Grand Rapids: Zondervan, 1991), 198.
4. Cloud and Townsend, *Boundaries,* 103.
5. Ibid.
6. Leslie B. Flynn, *How to Survive in the Ministry* (Grand Rapids: Kregel, 1992), 122.
7. Henri J. M. Nouwen, *The Wounded Healer* (New York: Doubleday, 1972), 82.

Chapter 9

1. H. B. London and Neil B. Wiseman, *Married to a Pastor: How to Stay Happily Married in Ministry* (Ventura, CA: Regal Books, 1999), 44–45.
2. Linda Riley, "When Your Minister-Husband Needs Help," published by Called Together Ministries, Torrance, California, 1987.
3. Janice Hildreth, *Pastor'sWife.com,* vol. 8, no. 7, July 2001.

Chapter 10

1. Ideas listed are from a compilation of my own notes as well as the following: *Heart to Heart with Pastors' Wives,* compiled by Lynne Dugan (Ventura, CA: Regal Books, 1994), appendix 3, 171–74; and Linda Riley, "Support for Your Support Group," published by Called Together Ministries, Torrance, California, 1997.

Chapter 11

1. Jill Briscoe, *Renewal on the Run* (Wheaton, IL: Harold Shaw, 1992), 63.
2. Ibid.
3. For further reading, see Barbara Johnson, *Pack Up Your Gloomees in a Great Big Box, Then Sit on the Lid and Laugh!* (Dallas: Word, 1993), chap. 5, "Life Is a Sexually Transmitted, Terminal Disease."
4. Al Miles, *Domestic Violence: What Every Pastor Needs to Know* (Minneapolis: Augsburg Fortress, 2000), taken from chapter 2 and the conclusion.

We want to hear from you. Please send your comments about this book to us in care of the address below. Thank you.

GRAND RAPIDS, MICHIGAN 49530 USA

WWW.ZONDERVAN.COM